C000228196

THE
PIANO PLAYER
of
BUDAPEST

THE
PIANO PLAYER
of
BUDAPEST

ROXANNE DE BASTION

ROBINSON

ROBINSON

First published in Great Britain in 2024 by Robinson

1 3 5 7 9 10 8 6 4 2

Copyright © Roxanne de Bastion, 2024
Photo author's own
Family tree by Liane Payne

The moral right of the author has been asserted.

All rights reserved.
No part of this publication may be reproduced, stored in a retrieval system,
or transmitted, in any form, or by any means, without the prior permission in
writing of the publisher, nor be otherwise circulated in any form of binding or
cover other than that in which it is published and without a similar condition
including this condition being imposed on the subsequent purchaser.

A CIP catalogue record for this book
is available from the British Library.

ISBN: 978-1-47214-784-4 (hardcover)
ISBN: 978-1-47214-785-1 (trade paperback)

Typeset in Adobe Garamond by Hewer Text UK Ltd, Edinburgh
Printed and bound in Great Britain by Clays Ltd, Elcograf S.p.A.

Papers used by Robinson are from well-managed
forests and other responsible sources.

Robinson
An imprint of
Little, Brown Book Group
Carmelite House
50 Victoria Embankment
London EC4Y 0DZ

An Hachette UK Company
www.hachette.co.uk

www.littlebrown.co.uk

For Richard

to those who struggle to know
where to call home
and which language is their own
to all who carry within them an ancient fear
and a sense of injustice
who may be feeling those things now
more than ever

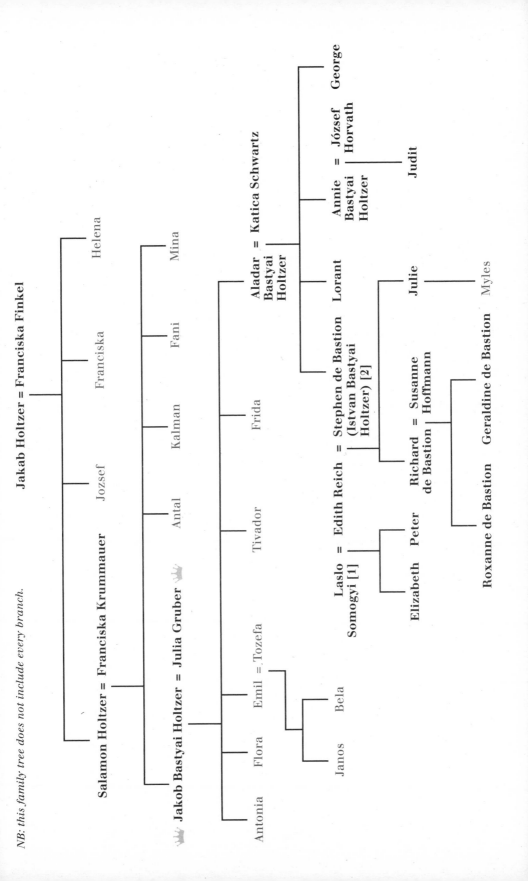

NB: this family tree does not include every branch.

Jakab Holtzer = Franciska Finkel

Helena

Franciska

Jozsef

Salamon Holtzer = Franciska Krummauer

Mina

Fani

Kalman

Antal

Jakob Bastyai Holtzer = Julia Gruber

Frida

Tivador

Antonia   Flora   Emil = Tozefa

Janos   Bela

Aladar = Katica Schwartz
Bastyai
Holtzer   Lorant

Stephen de Bastion
(Istvan Bastyai
Holtzer) [2]

Annie = József
Bastyai   Horvath
Holtzer

George

Judit

Julie

Laslo = Edith Reich [1]
Somogyi

Elizabeth   Peter

Richard = Susanne
de Bastion   Hoffmann

Roxanne de Bastion   Geraldine de Bastion   Myles

Contents

My Darling Children

Berlin 2020

My family has a piano. It has tiny marks on the top right corner where my dad used to gnaw at the wood with his baby teeth. Years later, while he played his compositions, I'd play underneath it, soaking up the sounds before my hands were large enough to reach a fifth.

I'm sitting at that piano now and, if I stretch, my hands can just about reach an octave. I may be able to reach those eight whole notes, but I can't stretch my mind to comprehend that my dad has just died.

He slipped away in this living room, the piano standing idly by as another of its custodians moved on. The intensity of the last few weeks has been replaced now with quiet – my dad never wanted to be a burden to anyone. And so he chose a polite moment to die, a rare minute when none of us – not my mum, my sister, our partners or myself – was in the room with him. It was just him and the piano.

The piano predates my memory. It had always been with us and, to a certain degree, I've taken its existence and its companionship for granted. But a loss this enormous paints everything in a new, harsher light. As I look at our piano now, I am suddenly so much more aware of its age. It's not shiny and black-lacquered as most pianos are. Instead, it's an aged, matt, wooden brown and is covered with lighter patches where the sun has shone on it through the blinds, like sunspots on an old man's face. The thin ivory keys feel weathered from touch, and above them, faded golden lettering spells out the make: Blüthner. It looks as though it should be in a museum, but it's in my parents' prefab house in the suburbs of Berlin, where I was raised.

On special occasions, my dad would open the top panel of this baby grand piano. To my younger self that was the most magical transformation to witness: for within this instrument, hidden away, was a secret universe – golden harp-like strings held down by light, wooden hammers and a slim, dark plinth on each end, to prop up its top panel to reveal the bright inners. Open, the sound would be brighter; it would sing out, somehow more youthful and vibrant.

Most of the time, the piano would sit, calmly and defiantly. It has a kind authority, allowing toddlers to thrash at its keys with sticky fingers. It is quietly encouraging, inviting any artist, no matter how proficient or amateur, to engage and create. There's something about our piano that brings out the best in its players and in my family – there have been four generations of them.

Family legend has it that my great-grandfather, Aladar, bought this piano in 1905, in Hungary, as an engagement gift for his wife-to-be, Katica. She, in turn, passed it on to her son, Stephen, and, when he died, it came here.

I can play, but not like my dad. Now he's gone, it'll be my job to take care of the piano. I'm a singer-songwriter, living in London in the age of music streaming, and I wonder whether I'll ever be able to afford a home big enough to house it. I imagine a crane trying to lift it into my rental flat and I wonder what my landlord would say. I'm good at songwriting and singing, but I'll never be able to improvise as beautifully or to play the piano like my dad with his perfect pitch and sensitivity – the ideal combination of head and heart. I feel lost now that he's not sat next to me any more to ground my lofty right-hand melodies with his comforting bass notes.

There are more unusual objects in this house. An array of family portraits line the walls of our home. The largest portrait is hanging right above the piano. It's a dark, rectangular painting of a young, glamorous-looking woman. She's got short, dark, wavy hair; a rosy-cheeked, heart-shaped face and small, round, shiny eyes. Her impressive, silver-grey gown is draped with a dark fur wrap, revealing a bare shoulder. She's wearing a long pearl necklace, matching earrings and a corresponding bracelet. Her smile is a mixture of coquettishness and boredom. I imagine she will have wanted to look good in the portrait but was most likely getting a little tired of sitting for it.

On the piano, stands a little black-and-white photograph of a young man with his hands resting on the same piano keys that I'm sitting in front of. He's wearing a tailored suit jacket. From underneath it pops a crisp white shirt. His facial expression is serene, his gaze turned downwards.

The portraits were always a talking point whenever anyone came over for the first time. None of my friends had paintings of dead relatives on their walls. They were quite the hit at sleepover parties when I was little, my friends pretending the framed faces were haunted and might come to life while we were tucked up in our sleeping bags.

'Is your family rich?' a girl once asked me in school when I said we had a grand piano at home.

'No. I think we used to be a long time ago,' I replied at the age of seven.

The grandeur of the portraits and the piano are at stark odds with their surroundings. My mother is a retired social worker; my dad, whom I struggle to speak of in the past tense, a musician with various part-time teaching jobs. He'd have phases in-between and around teaching music when he would gig, in various bands or as a solo singer-songwriter. My parents are children of the sixties and seventies: liberal, impulsive, very much not business or career orientated. Still, they argued a lot about money. In a way, the baby grand piano and the family portraits *were* haunted. They were ghosts of a bygone era, hinting at fortunes lost.

The root note of any musical key is referred to as 'home'. In a song, 'home' is an anchor. When we hear it, we intuitively feel a sense of having arrived, or being safe. I never had to ask myself what I wanted to do with my life. As vague as my understanding was of where I came from, I was always certain about where I was going. I decided at the age of four, after being introduced to The Beatles, that I was going to make music. I was obsessed with writing my own songs and made my first clumsy attempts on our piano, mimicking my dad and John Lennon in equal measure.

Outside of that musical context, home has been harder to find. Wherever I am, I am always the foreigner. I was born here in Berlin, as was my mother. My dad was born in the West Midlands, as was my sister. As a family, we moved back and forth, neither country feeling a perfect fit for us, but liberal Berlin ultimately winning over the very conservative West Midlands, England. My mother could never get used to seeing her children in uniform, nor that asking for a second opinion at the doctors seemed to be frowned upon.

Straddling two cultures and speaking two languages to the same degree of proficiency brings with it a unique set of advantages and disadvantages. I can detach the sound of a word from its meaning. As a songwriter, I wouldn't want to miss that. Comparing idioms is a delight (in German, we dance around the hot porridge, as opposed to the more violent beating around the bush). But there is a limit to how fully I can express myself in either language, and when I'm with someone who only identifies with either one of those cultures and languages, a side of me always remains in the shadows.

And then, in addition to the German and the British, there is this third, hidden layer to my identity, the heirlooms and the hearsay. The portraits, the piano, they speak their own language, further complicating my answer to the frequently asked question: 'Where are you from?' 'Home' as in middle C is a much easier concept for me.

I knew from an early age that the artefacts in our home – the piano and the portraits – were unusual. It took a little longer for me to realise that it was also unusual to have distant relatives dotted around the globe. When I was little I assumed everyone had an assortment of relations in disparate corners of the world, such as Canada, the US and Australia. I thought little on why we were all so far apart. The older relatives on my dad's side of the family all spoke with a different accent. They all have more than one nationality. They all have something about them that screams 'foreign'.

Most of those relatives have long since passed, but I remember my grandmother and my Great-uncle Lorant speaking Hungarian with one another. To me, it sounded like a fantastical back and forth of animated mystery. The one stoic anchor, tying my family to its roots, is my dad's cousin Judit. She divides her time between Hungary and

Sweden. Her accent is different yet again – when she speaks, her English is a rather distinct mix of her native and elected homes. With Berlin being a good halfway point between them, she would visit us often. She would always greet my dad in that secret, lost language: 'Szervusz dragam.' Although the language was secret to him, too, he knew her words meant, 'Hello, my sweet darling.'

I don't remember when I learned that my father's family, those faces in the paintings and photographs, were Jewish. I was always somehow aware of the fact, as if it was a shade of paint blending in the background of their portraits. Overall, there was very little discussion as to what being Jewish even meant, other than a vague notion that it was somehow the reason why we, as a family, found ourselves in a very different place, physically and metaphorically, two generations on.

My dad never identified as Jewish, no matter how much his cousin Judit insisted that he was just that, whether he liked it or not. If anything, he'd emphasise that even my grandparents and great-grandparents never practised Judaism. We grew up in a household without prescribed religion. My mother was keen to let my sister and me grow to an age where we could make up our own minds about whether we wanted to go to any kind of church. Inevitably, we didn't. My dad's attitude towards religion was more complex. He was equally, if not more emphatically, keen that we should live our lives without a religious label, but for reasons even he didn't fully understand until much later. It took my dad a life-time to accept and understand that he was holding a lot of inher-ited fear within him. In the end, his ardent attempts to escape 'being Jewish' were futile: he died on Yom Kippur, the holiest day in the Jewish calendar.

In my dad's house, there are drawers and boxes filled with old cassette tapes, CDs, letters, documents, books and photographs. He jokingly christened himself 'Richard the Recorder' and garnered a reputation for being the custodian of all things family history. Whenever an older family member passed away, the default response would be, 'Well, Richard will take this.' Every time his sister, my Aunt Julie, went through a decluttering phase – and they were so frequent, I always wondered how there could possibly be any clutter left to discard – she'd post stacks of documents and photographs to my dad, along with a scribbled note in flamboyant cursive: *Darlings – here are photos of Mummy and Daddy on holiday and some other faces I don't recognise – may they bring you joy. Love, Julie.*

For a large portion of her life, my aunt felt physical belongings, especially those relating to family history, were a burden.

My older sister and I are daunted by the fact that our dad's life is now a part of that growing family history, his documents, photographs and belongings stored together with those of his parents and those who came before them. He had a knack for accumulating random bits and pieces and storing them in unlikely places, which makes going through his things an emotional minefield. How can I throw away a telephone bill if there are lyric ideas scribbled on the back? I open a tiny box that's hidden away at the back of a drawer – it contains a pebble, a paper clip and a tooth: 'Oh yeah! Don't you know that story?' My sister laughs at my perturbed facial expression, and we pause our sorting process for her to fill me in. Every time neither of us knows the story to a mystery assortment of things, we cry and wish we'd listened more or asked more or remembered better.

I open the drawers, one by one, of an industrial-looking filing cabinet that's propping up the desk. It's filled with perfectly stacked cassette tapes. Some are blank or scrawled upon in a handwriting I don't recognise. Most of them are meticulously labelled in my dad's handwriting, which is not cursive like his sister's. His is neat, uniform, and it fills me with a warmth when I see it:

Stephen – The Rainbow Rooms, 1957
Stephen – 1907–1920
Stephen – In a Sentimental Mood
Stephen tells his war story – Part 1
Stephen tells his war story – Part 2
Stephen tells his war story – Part 3

In these early days of grieving, I have so many seemingly random, small thoughts. Upon discovering the cassette tapes, I am overcome with emotions: not curiosity over the contents or joy at how much there is to discover, but wonder at how neatly the cassettes are stacked and how well organised the drawers are. In that moment, I feel hopelessly inadequate. Unlike my dad, I am no good at keeping things nice and orderly.

Later that night, I listen to one of the unmarked tapes and I come across the familiar sound of our piano. It has a uniquely warm, soft tone. The player is not my dad, though. The recording sounds too old and the playing is too flowery, too classical, to be his.

I never got to know Stephen, my grandfather, the dapper man in the photograph on top of the Blüthner. To me, he is the perfect enigma. I did meet him once, but I was just a few months old, incapable of forming a lasting memory of my own. And so I soaked up other people's stories and impressions of him, but they were confusing and painted a dichotomous picture.

In more recent photos, capturing him in the orange-and-brown-tinted nineteen seventies and early eighties, he looks vulnerable. His face is kinder than in the earlier black-and-white versions, but I feel the effort it takes him to just sit in his armchair and smile through the photo. The photograph of him playing the piano shows a serene confidence. He has what I would call 'performer eyes': a look that goes out into the room, above people's heads, focusing on nothing in particular but giving everyone in the room a feeling of being seen. I love this version of my grandfather.

The cassette I'm listening to is a copy of a Ferrograph recording made in 1954. Stephen is playing a composition of his called 'An Old Mill is Dreaming'. Perchance, it is the only composition of his that I am familiar with. Although, through this lens of raw and jagged grief, it feels like I'm hearing it for the first time.

It starts out menacingly low and slow. It's full of sorrow, and mirrors my state of mind perfectly. Then, Stephen delicately sweeps across the keys to convey a sound we might hear in an old movie to suggest the protagonist is falling asleep. He guides the listener seamlessly through an array of emotions, from romance to chaos, drama to resolve. When the song finishes, there is a click and then a voice appears. Stephen must have recorded over a previous take – there is a ghost piano, whirling away in the background underneath his words. With modern-day recording technology this would be an easy thing to do: I'd record two separate tracks digitally, one with my piano playing, another with my spoken message, and simply stack them on top of one another using software, adjusting the volume of each individual track. In 1954, this must have been achieved by a sheer quirk of fate. Somehow, when Stephen rewound the physical tape and recorded his message on to it, it must have not fully erased what was on that tape. As if by magic, the ghost piano perfectly underlined his message:

The story is about an old mill who stood alone, deserted, in a field. His voice is deep and the tape is grainy. He has a thick, Hungarian accent that elongates the 'o' in 'alone'.

On a summer night, when it was full moon, he was dreaming that he was young again. He sang a love song of his youth, and he felt his wheels going round and round, faster and faster and he was singing and rejoicing with all his heart. Suddenly, the dream has passed, but he did not want to believe it. He wanted to carry on, to be young. He forced his wheels to turn and turn again, but the wheels could not . . . any more. They stopped moving. And so, the old mill stood still again in the moonlight and gave up all hope as he realised that youth comes never back.

My dad couldn't keep his wheels spinning in the end. Unlike the old mill, though, he never lost his youth. My thoughts are interrupted by a further click on the tape. There was that voice again: *My darling children. I have finished now my story. Tomorrow is Richard's seventh birthday. May God give you and your darling little sister Julika, both of you, health and happiness your whole life.*

As I listen to my grandfather wish my dad a happy birthday, time stands still. I reach through it and hug that seven-year-old boy. Then, I think more on that deep, foreign-sounding voice. I wonder what story he is telling. 'An Old Mill is Dreaming' seems to contain a whole life within its nine minutes. A life full of rude interruptions.

I know that he was a charming man, although some describe him as difficult. I'm told that he could be harsh in tone and verbally cruel. I know that he was a pianist and found some success before the war. I know that he was sent to Russia as a forced labourer and that he somehow survived that, as well as imprisonment in a concentration camp. I know that he forbade my father to ever return to Hungary – a wish he upheld until Stephen was no longer alive. I know that Stephen recorded what he experienced during the war on to cassette tapes. I've never felt ready to hear it. I know that when he emigrated to England in 1948, 'Istvan' became 'Stephen'. He changed our family name from the Hungarian 'Bastyai Holtzer' to the rather French-sounding 'de Bastion'. I always thought that said a lot about him. He must have been weary enough to want to assimilate, but flamboyant and proud enough to not want to blend in entirely. Ever since I started performing, people have assumed that de Bastion was a stage name and, in a way, it is – just one created for me, two generations ago.

Thinking on all the coincidences, all the decisions, the chance meetings, the left turns that lead to our individual existence can be overwhelming. For second- and third-generation survivors of the Holocaust, this is amplified. Even as I type that last sentence, I feel the residue of my dad's trauma course through my veins and slow down my fingertips. He would never call himself a second-generation survivor out loud. He would not use the word Holocaust and tie it to himself and his identity in any way. But I have the gift of distance. And in my grief, I have a growing longing for connection, to find out more about those missing puzzle pieces to my identity. I want to get to know my grandfather and explore how much of myself and my dad I find in him. I want to know what happened and who we were, before we were 'foreign'. My dad would identify as a musician and a creator. He would see the piano as an accepted, positive part of himself, tying him to his family's tumultuous past. So that is where I'll begin. I want to unearth the stories our piano has to tell about its most prodigal player and how it, along with him, survived.

And so, I pack the cassette tapes, photo albums and letters and take them back to England. Back in my flat, I press play on the next cassette: 'Stephen tells his war story – Part 1'.

PART ONE

Music

CHAPTER 1

Send Me a Wire

Music is a calling and twenty-nine-year-old Stephen de Bastion, or Istvan Bastyai Holtzer as he was then, has always felt it within him. Officially, Stephen works for his parents, taking care of bookkeeping and other administrative tasks in the family textile firm. Actually, he's somewhat of a professional socialite, with infectious charm and an insatiable passion for playing the piano.

He is the eldest of four children and had therefore felt it particularly embarrassing to have recently had to move back home with his parents after suffering a bitter divorce from a short and mutually loveless marriage. It has left him with a bruised ego and a readiness to pursue passions.

One might think that living with his family would cramp this eligible bachelor's style, but this is no ordinary abode. His family own the apartment block on the corner of the aptly named St Stephen's Square in central Budapest. His parents' apartment takes up the entirety of the third floor. It looks straight onto St Stephen's Basilica, a neoclassical church, which casts a magnificent light reflected from the pale stone into the large, bay window at the rounded front of the building. The seventeen rooms of the apartment boast a stately interior with rich fabric wallpaper, fine drapery, beautifully crafted furniture, oil paintings and chandeliers. Amid such opulence, the risk of a run-in with his mother or father after a late night is low. His sister Annie has just moved in with her new husband – a newly framed photograph of her with her mother, Katica, and brothers, Stephen and Lorant, at the wedding hangs in the entrance hall of the apartment – and the youngest brother George is away at university. Stephen practically has the entire place to himself.

He can almost always be found in one particular room. Tucked away at the back of the building is a drawing room, which the family uses for entertaining. This is where they keep the Blüthner baby grand piano. As far back as Stephen's memory can stretch, it has always been a part of their household and playing it has always been his favourite pastime. As a child, he would entertain himself for hours on end playing, learning and composing. Even now in adulthood, it is part of his everyday – he plays the Blüthner for an hour after having lunch with his parents, daydreams his way through the afternoon shift and then heads out into the evening for more music.

Budapest is bursting with a youthful exuberance. One of the largest cities in central Europe, it had grown into a vibrant cultural hub, its shine christening the city 'the pearl of the Danube'. Budapest is a city of two halves, Buda and Pest, straddling the Danube River and connected by several bridges. While the west side of town offers the more beautiful landscape, with hills rolling south towards the sea, the east side, on which Stephen finds himself, is alive with theatre, music, drink and a raucous nightlife. Across both, there is an air of wellbeing, of abundance and optimism.

Stephen feels at home in Pest, among the artists and intellectuals frequenting the many coffee bars and high-society hangouts; he is intent on making the most of his newly regained freedom.

*　　*　　*

One evening in 1936, Stephen joins a group of friends at one of Budapest's most elegant nightclubs. He is wearing a buttoned-down silk shirt underneath a black dinner jacket and is sitting at a crowded round table laden with ashtrays and half-empty glasses. He tunes out of the animated conversation around him. While his friends continue to swill the wine in their glasses and gesticulate with their cigarette holders, heads tilted towards one another as they share anecdotes and flirtations, Stephen shifts his gaze to the piano player across the room.

Here at the Parisien Grill, Budapest's young and fashionable show off their finery, listen to live music, dance, drink and watch cabaret and dance performances into the early hours. The club is vast and expands across two floors. In the centre of the room, the dance floor shimmers underneath the light of chunky, Art Deco chandeliers. Beautifully winding staircases with ornately carved wooden banisters run from either side of the stage, connecting the lower floor with the upper balcony – both of which are lined with small, round tables and chairs. There's hardly ever a free seat to be found. Today, there's no dance or cabaret performance – just the usual house band playing.

The pianist concludes a nondescript waltz, closes the lid of the instrument and gets up to take his scheduled break. Stephen seizes the moment, as he often would, abandoning his drink and motioning with one hand for his friends to follow him as he shuffles across the dance floor towards the white grand piano. With a brief approval-seeking nod to the staff behind the bar, Stephen sits at the piano, opens the lid and starts playing. Beautifully improvised melodies weave their way around a medley of themes from popular songs of the day. A couple of his friends form a half-circle around the piano and other bar goers are quick to take note and follow suit. It's easy for Stephen to impress people with his playing. It's not common to see someone play without sheet music and Stephen plays freely, from memory and with his whole heart. It's his party trick and it works every time.

'Istvan, that was so beautiful . . .' George, one of his acquaintances, pours Stephen another glass of wine as he sits back down at the table after his impromptu performance.

Acknowledging the compliment, Stephen places a hand on his friend's shoulder, and re-directs the conversation: 'So,' he says to George, 'tell us what fascinating adventures you've been up to today.'

'Oh!' George exclaims with a smile. 'Today I went to the police to pick up my passport. My trio has just been hired to perform at the Küchlin Theatre in Basel. Me, my pianist and drummer, we're moving to Switzerland next month!'

A clinking of glasses and a flurry of good wishes spill across the table.

'Well, if that pianist of yours doesn't work out,' Stephen replies with a raised eyebrow, trying to hide the spark that, in that very second, has ignited within him, 'send me a wire.'

CHAPTER 2

And So It Was

When my dad was little, he attempted to write his life story. He didn't get very far, scrawling in his notebook, but his opening words carry an aching profundity that only the innocence of childhood can bring: 'I was born laughing.'

The same could not be said of Stephen, who was told by his mother Katica that he had refused to come into this world. On 19 May 1907, he was eventually pulled out of her with metal tongs after days of labouring, the difficult birth of her firstborn foreboding that life ahead would not be as blessed as the family's luxurious surroundings might suggest. When he finally arrived, his nose was completely flat, which frightened the new mother. Apparently, she had remarked that it was a good thing Stephen was not a girl; he would be all right in this world, even without a nose. The doctor was quick to reassure her that this was, in fact, normal for a newborn and that within a few days, her child would have a perfectly fine nose.

And so it was! Stephen shares in his tapes. *I can still be proud of my nose, which is neither too crooked nor too long. In my opinion it is a nice nose.*

A couple of years after his arrival, his mother gave birth to his twin brothers, Lorant and Aladar, followed by his sister Annie and, finally, baby brother George. The twins were sickly children and Aladar died an infant's death. My Great-uncle Lorant would joke his entire life that he could never really be sure if he was in fact himself or his twin brother, as a careless nanny could have easily switched the two without anyone noticing.

The family was running a successful textile business and lived a very comfortable life. In their raised bungalow in Szeged was a library, a saloon where Katica and Aladar would entertain guests, not least with the help of the Blüthner piano, a dining hall, a kitchen and servants' quarters, as well as several bedrooms. Behind the house, Aladar kept a horse in a stable, along with a pen of hunting pigeons. The staff included a coachman and his wife, a cook, a maid and a nanny to tend to the children – or a Fräulein, as Stephen would refer to them, as they would usually be German.

I wasn't a friendly or communicative young boy.

Stephen doesn't share many stories of his childhood. His recollections of his early years include seemingly random, inconsequential memories, yet I can't help but attribute meaning to every single one; each holding a clue to the kind of person he truly was. In one of these fragmented memories, Stephen is walking through town with his Aunt Antonia. They run into the local rabbi. A man of great social stature, he wasn't just a spiritual leader, but also sat in the House of Magnates, the Hungarian House of Lords. Too shy to speak when asked to introduce himself, Stephen instead kicked the rabbi in the shin. Antonia was mortified and her adult embarrassment clung to Stephen's being enough for the story to be retold in this tape over half a century later. Don't we all have those early memories that stick to us like goosegrass? When I was three years old I ran into the kitchen in a fit of rage (what a three-year-old has to be raging against, I do not know), grabbed a full carton of milk out of the fridge and, looking my mother straight in the eyes, smashed it down on the floor, where it burst open, milk spilling into the cracks of the linoleum. My mother tells this story laughing, but when she does, a combination of embarrassment and an age-old rage courses through my veins as hot, prickly tears shimmer across my eyes. Crying over spilt milk.

There's a portrait of Stephen as a little boy, currently hanging in my Aunt Julie's council flat in the West Midlands, that was never finished. In it, Stephen is posing, resting his chin on a balled-up little fist, sitting cross-legged on a red wicker chair. His face wears a pained expression of impatience. I can just imagine him squirming in that chair as the pattern of the wicker leaves uncomfortable imprints on his knees, begging for the ordeal to be over, for playtime to begin. Sitting still for hours while a stranger paints you for reasons you don't understand does sound like torture for a little boy. I can imagine an older relative – or more likely a nanny – snapping back at him, telling him that he was not a friendly child.

Stephen's happier early childhood memories include family holidays. The entire clan, including grandparents, aunts, uncles and cousins, would gather regularly, either in a thermal spa location such as Marienbad or Franzensbad in Czechoslovakia or for a coastal holiday by the Adriatic Sea to spend quality time together. For the children, this meant playing war games. Stephen recalls one incident where, unbeknownst to him, the other cousins had agreed to come dressed up as soldiers. Stephen, unhappy to be the only one wearing a simple striped T-shirt – no helmet or pretend army jacket in sight – decided to solve the issue by simply being the first fatality, dropping to the ground and lying still until the bloody battle of the holiday house reached its conclusion.

I hear in his voice that he's still pleased with this particular example of problem-solving and amused by his younger self. Stephen wasn't one to sulk or feel slighted. He enjoyed finding loopholes in the system. He took any opportunity to be creative and to stand out by doing things his own way.

Whether in play or reality, war was a harsh fixture of Stephen's life. He was only seven years old when the First World War broke out and his father Aladar was sent to fight at the Serbian front. The family are patriotic and Aladar, though a gentle man, saw defending Hungary as his duty. Suddenly, Katica found herself running the business, with little time to tend to the children. Whether it was the weight of change or simply a stroke of bad luck, Stephen fell seriously ill. He struggled to breathe and developed a dangerously high fever. It got so bad that the doctor said there was little hope and was ready to declare him dead. Refusing to lose another child, particularly her beloved firstborn, Katica took it upon herself to find a remedy for her son, the first of many times she'd go into battle for her eldest. It was the fourth doctor who finally diagnosed him with diphtheria (seven years before the epidemic would reach its peak) and intubated him so he could breathe more easily. For weeks, Stephen was confined to a bedroom, draped in sea-salt-soaked sheets to aid his breathing and healing. When he made a full recovery, his mother gifted him a complete miniature Hungarian soldier's uniform. The 'Hussar' uniform consisted of red trousers, a red cap and a navy blue jacket. With patriotic pride, Stephen, in uniform, would play at home, arranging his lead soldiers, playing out in innocence a fictional version of what his father was experiencing in gruesome reality. At least in pretend battle, Stephen would never be underdressed again.

Stephen wasn't a great student, although he was at least 'much better than Lorant!', as he's quick to interject on the subject. He and his younger brothers attended the Piarista Gymnasium, a strict Catholic school. Stephen got through, by the skin of his teeth, and not without the occasional scrap with fellow pupils or those of the rivalling school. He was athletic and not afraid to pull a punch to defend himself: *Maybe I was by nature a tough boy*, he reflects.

If Stephen was a tough boy, it didn't show in his piano playing. With great sensitivity and creativity, he improvised from an early age. The younger siblings loved gathering around the piano, listening to their mother and brother play Chopin together. Playing and enjoying music must have been a welcome distraction from worrying about Aladar as he fought, now on the Italian front.

After four years of deployment, Aladar was sent home early due to his worsening arthritis and soon after, the war was lost. There was much bitterness at the loss of so many soldiers' lives and the perceived futility of it all. A general feeling of unrest and a desire for change was in the air.

For a while, though, life continued peacefully in Szeged.

Because Stephen showed such skill and enthusiasm for the piano, his maternal grandfather Gustav thought it would be a good idea to encourage his other grandchildren to take up music. He arranged for Annie to have singing lessons, bought Lorant a cello and George a violin. Along with these gifts, he also sent the family a pet – a small, yellow canary. While Annie proved to have a beautiful singing voice and George dutifully learned violin, Lorant was far more interested in the little creature living in the brass cage than the instrument left listlessly in the corner of the dining room. Much like his father, his passion was for animals and the outdoors. During the weekends, dividing parental duties became easy – every Sunday, Aladar would take Lorant with him to ride the horses, to race pigeons and to visit the shooting range, while Katica stayed indoors to play music and paint with Stephen, Annie and George.

In 1923, though, the family relocated closer to Aladar's parents, swapping the bungalow in Szeged for the apartment in Budapest. It must have been exciting for Stephen to move to the country's capital just as his adult life began: he was sixteen. While his younger siblings were eagerly eyeing up the toys in the conveniently located toy shop in the square by their apartment block, Stephen perused the shiny gramophone records.

In music, tension is a term that refers to the anticipation music creates in the listener's mind for relaxation or release. A piano player might create it, for example, through gradual motion, working their way towards a higher or lower pitch, or by artfully increasing in dynamics or skilfully toying with a push and pull between consonance and dissonance. Stephen's young adult life was defined by such a tension – a soft and constant tug of war between vocation and expectation.

Bowing to his father's will, Stephen studied textile and machine engineering. He showed precious little interest in either (*I never liked nor understood machines and in Szeged, in these times, you could hardly even see a motorcar!*), but started his studies at Zurich's prestigious polytechnic university regardless.

My nature directed me in the opposite direction, which was music – that, to me, was easy to follow.

At university, Stephen's single-mindedness grew and time away with peers only strengthened his resolve. He soaked up all that student life had to offer, save for actually attending the classes. He would often walk past fellow students in the hallway – they were heading to morning lectures and he was heading to bed, returning from a night of partying and music making.

Stephen did involve himself in various sport activities the university had to offer. Skilled at tennis and boxing, he started competing. He took part in the summer circuit championships around Switzerland in both disciplines, representing the university he barely attended. It is clear in his retelling that Stephen took great pride in his physical fitness. He shares that Katica and Aladar even came to cheer him on in the finals. It is a proud moment he looks back on fondly.

With regards to his studies, Stephen admits, *I was not interested, and so I failed*, before concluding: *I had three wonderful years in Zürich*.

It had all come to a head when Aladar paid Stephen a surprise visit only to find him asleep, passed out in an armchair, clearly wearing the suit he had worn the night before, with an empty wine bottle beside him. Once he had managed to get his son up and dressed and, after a talking-to, he asked Stephen to give him a tour of the university. Stephen struggled even to find the way from his lodging to the lecture rooms, but he could show Aladar every coffee shop, restaurant or nightclub around town. Stephen's photograph was hanging in the windows of the restaurants and coffee houses, advertising his weekly performances. After this visit, Aladar capitulated, finally realising that he was wasting his money on the expensive textile course.

The failed studies are followed up with internships in wholesale businesses in London and Paris. Stephen in his twenties displayed youthful arrogance, spending more of his energy on his musical endeavours than on various jobs and tasks he deemed undeserving of his talents.

His time in London was typical of young Stephen, unaware of how privileged he was. Aladar funded his lifestyle abroad, providing him with a very generous £20 a month. For context, Mr Spielman, the landlord at the flat Stephen boarded in, a two-bedroom property in Islington near Arsenal's football ground, Highbury, earned just £3 a week. Stephen repaid Mr Spielman's hospitality by having an affair with his wife.

Mr Spielman was a radio ham and soon retired to his room for his passion – and Mrs Spielman spent her passion with me. She was a pretty lively Irish girl. Mr Spielman was Polish. Heaven knows what they found in each other to get married.

He showed similar hubris at his job. Stephen had been gifted an internship via Aladar's business connections at a textile company called Mullen Brothers. By the third week, he grew frustrated that many of his duties were menial, such as carrying heavy suitcases full of blankets and scarves in and out of shops along a bustling Oxford Street.

I went to Mr Mullen and told him I did not come to him as a porter, but to study export/import! So we parted amicably.

For Stephen, it was only ever about his music. It was his passion, his drive and invention that led him to knock on the doors of music publishing companies in London's Denmark Street.

I went to Dix Publishing Group and presented my own composition and my own lyrics. It was called 'Up and Down the Scale of Life'. He liked it, accepted it and published it. I got fifty pounds as performing rights – an enormous achievement! A little Hungarian boy of around twenty-three against all the sharks from Denmark Street.

Stephen's composition was played on the radio and was even performed by a famous band leader of the day, Jack Payne. As exciting as this was at the time, it didn't prove to be the career stepping stone that he had hoped for.

After nearly six years abroad, Stephen returns to Budapest. His mother, in particular, had missed him dearly during his time away and, when he returns to the family apartment, she eagerly ushers him into the living room where his father is already waiting for him. 'What did you learn? Tell us everything,' she asks.

'I'll show you!' Stephen exclaims, full of youthful arrogance, as he rushes to the piano. He sits down and starts playing the Charleston.

CHAPTER 3

Help, I Inherited!

Some ambitions are too sacred to voice out loud. As much as he wanted to keep his parents happy, privately, Stephen always wanted to be a professional player. On one particular night out, just before his twenties come to a close, a chance meeting finally offers a glimmer of hope that this secret wish may become a reality.

Stephen is out at his most frequented spot, the Anglo-Hungarian Society. Once or twice every week, he spends his evenings here, soaking up the opulence of the social club. Bathing in the light of spectacular chandeliers, Hungarian bohemians mingle on a dance floor lined with ornate furniture; waiters in full uniform serve drinks and canapés. His fondness for this establishment hasn't dimmed, despite the fact that it was here where he met his now ex-wife shortly after he returned from his time abroad, just over two years ago. It had seemed so good on paper – 'Baba', which was her nickname and means 'Doll' in Hungarian, was young, pretty and the daughter of a brandy manufacturer, who was keen for her to marry into a reputable family such as the Holtzers. For Baba, though, Stephen proved to be a less than an ideal partner, his musical passion far outweighing his drive in business. Shortly after their wedding, she started an affair with a local drinks distributor, before finally asking for a divorce and leaving Stephen for a man ten years his senior.

He thinks of her briefly before knocking back a cognac by the bar. Today, he feels it has all been for the best and is determined to embrace his freedom to the fullest. In that moment, Stephen sees the unmanned grand piano nestled in the far right of the hall. He slides on to the velvet-covered piano stool and leaps into a playfully syncopated version of 'Pennies from Heaven'. When he reaches the part in the song where Bing Crosby sings 'That's what storms are made for. And you shouldn't be afraid for', he slows it down drastically and includes flowery, improvised scales in between the chords. At this precise moment, Stephen spies a striking woman wearing a floor-length, cream-coloured gown and a light fur coat walking from the crowded bar directly towards him. A master of soundtracking his surroundings, he cheekily and seamlessly transitions into a slow, embellished version of 'The Way You Look Tonight'.

'Now, why have I not heard you play before?'

Stephen, still playing, looks up at the woman and grins. With one more dramatic scale, he concludes his playing and jumps to his feet to meet Irene Agay.

Irene is already famous. In fact, she needn't have introduced herself; Stephen knows exactly who he's standing in front of. A Budapest native, Irene was a child stage and film actress who managed to grow her career into adulthood. Her most recent role, starring in the hit play *Emma*, elevated her to a new level of adoration. She looks the part of a 1930s movie star: her short, golden-brown hair set neatly into pinned waves, and her heart-shaped face accentuated by thinly pencilled eyebrows and dramatically painted lips. After exchanging introductory pleasantries, she motions to the bar and says: 'Come, you must meet my husband!'

This takes Stephen somewhat by surprise, as he was certain Irene had been particularly flirtatious with him. Regardless, he follows her to the bar.

'Istvan,' she ushers him towards a tall, suited man, 'meet Istvan!'

His namesake, now standing before him with a warm smile and an outstretched hand, is film producer Istvan Székely. This Istvan is ten years his senior, his friendly demeanour underpinned with an air of gravitas. Like Irene, he's impeccably dressed. His face is framed with a pair of small, round spectacles and he's sporting a thick, dark brown moustache.

'Beautiful playing! Such sensitivity! Where did you study?'

This question always bodes well for Stephen. He knows that the honest answer – 'Oh, I didn't study music. I'm self-taught' – impresses. For him, this portion of small talk is far better rehearsed than any one of his compositions. The trio hit it off and stay out drinking and chatting until the first light of daybreak shimmers through the windows of the Anglo-Hungarian Society. That morning Stephen feels a peaceful euphoria as he walks home. The night had gone well and something exciting, he senses, is going to come of it.

Sure enough, not long after the encounter, Istvan offers Stephen the job of composing the music for his latest film, a romantic comedy called *Help, I Inherited!* ('Segítség örököltem'). It doesn't bother the filmmaker that Stephen struggles to transcribe his compositions; his creativity and character more than make up for his somewhat unorthodox approach.

On 2 August 1937, Stephen nervously adjusts his cravat in the hallway mirror, while his brother Lorant patiently waits for him by the front door.

'The driver is waiting and you're not going to get any handsomer,' he teases.

'Just as well, isn't it?' Stephen smiles back at him as he turns away from his reflection and follows his brother out the door and down the staircase, their echoing footsteps increasing Stephen's anticipation.

'Edes drágáim!' (Sweet ones!) Katica cups her head in her hands, admiring her boys and looking from them back at Aladar in a way parents do in a moment of pride – a dreamy 'Can you believe we made these?' kind of expression. While she is used to seeing her eldest dressed up, nature-loving Lorant is much more at home in the outdoors and is usually dressed in mud-stained leather jackets. Today, he's wearing a three-piece suit, coattails and all, and is sporting a large, top hat.

They climb into the car, which takes them to Budapest's Metro cinema, where tonight *Help, I Inherited!* is being premiered.

The Bastyai Holtzer family fit in perfectly with the sparkling starlets, actors, journalists and invited guests. Stephen introduces his family to Irene and Istvan, who gush flattering niceties about their son's talents to them. The director, actress and composer are ushered towards the red carpet for photos, and Katica, Aladar and Lorant head inside the cinema with the other guests to take their seats.

A flurry of nerves rush through Stephen as the cinema grows dark and the opening credits appear on the large screen before them, his music filling the room. He is grateful for the darkness, as he does not want to appear outwardly nervous. As the credits come to a close, much to his surprise, the audience break into spontaneous applause in appreciation of his composition – this, Stephen thinks, as he turns to Istvan, eyes wide, is going very well. Istvan gives him a pleased nod and Irene reaches over her husband and gives Stephen's upper arm an excited, tight squeeze.

Throughout the film, Stephen's music, as well as Irene's performance, evokes applause. As the final scene closes and the room grows
dark, the audience erupt once more into applause and jump to their
feet, giving the film a standing ovation.

Much later that night, once his family have left him at the party
after celebrating the success of the event, Stephen finds himself
sitting alone with Irene. Breaking a rare moment of silence, she says:
'Well, young composer, do you have a bachelor pad?'

Unusually flustered, Stephen is taken aback and stumbles over his
words.

'I'm, I'm sorry, I haven't.'

'Well, you had better get one; otherwise you won't be able to take
me home.'

Needless to say, my grandfather tells me in the tapes, his voice
bouncing, *that in twenty-four hours I had rented a flat. It was fully
furnished. I mean, I bought all the furniture necessary so her wish and
my wish were fulfilled.*

I'm on a train heading to another show as I'm listening to this,
and if I'd have just taken a sip of the take-away coffee that's resting
on the little plastic tray table in front of me, I would have undoubtedly spat it out. I take a moment to think on what exactly Stephen
deemed necessary furniture and wonder whether my grandfather's
first bachelor flat had anything in it other than a bed and whether
Katica and Aladar had questioned the very sudden move. Either
way, I suppose it's good to know that he did eventually move out of
his parents' home and into his own apartment, braving the big move
across the Danube from Pest over to Buda. I imagine that the criteria
for the flat was how quickly it was available and whether he could
afford the rent with his film score income – everything else will have

been secondary. I am both bemused and taken aback by the ease with which Stephen commits adultery. I listen to this part of the tape several times, to make sure I haven't misheard.

Stephen paints a rich picture of the high-flying love triangle – the actress, the producer and the composer, all glitzy stars out on the town, being photographed as celebrities of the film world, in Budapest's nightclubs, restaurants and cafés. To me, it is strangely endearing that Stephen wants to share this story both in the tapes as well as in his letters. There is of course an element of grandstanding, but more so, Stephen is composing his story, sprinkling a shimmering, right-hand melody as light relief and colour, before the lower, darker key change that is to come. He places his affair in the context of the Bohemian art world he felt so at home in:

The theatrical people are a creed on their own. No scruples, very natural and direct . . . when two people liked each other, they make love and that's all there is to it. Affairs can be of permanent nature, but just once is just the same. I hardly remember anyone who was sad, gloomy – but always optimistic, always smiling and friendly.

I have seen the film. It is accessible with a simple search, a record of our disparate pasts held online. I am mesmerised when I first see it and surprised that at least some of my grandfather's work, unbeknownst to me, exists in the public domain. The soundtrack comes roaring in, a drum roll followed by a dramatic blow of trumpets and woodwind instruments, as the black-and-white credits start to roll. There it is, in a cartoon-like font: 'Zene (music) by Istvan Bastyai'.

My sister and I begin to tackle some of the many boxes stored in my parents' attic. The largest of the boxes is filled with sheets of music notation, concert pamphlets and reviews, as well as stacks of cassettes full of Stephen's piano playing. I thumb through one of the many binders and see cuttings from Hungarian newspapers – a weathered yellow behind clear, protective plastic. Some of the cuttings have pen markings, circling certain paragraphs. The highlighted part of one *Help, I Inherited!* film review reads:

Istvan Székely did an admiral job as director. Istvan Bastyai, a new composer, introduced himself with great enthusiasm – a serious talent and definitely one to watch.

Another circled paragraph on a different cutting reads:

The film also introduced a new composer named Istvan Bastyai. He is a skilful musician whose two compositions will certainly quickly become popular on the street.

The review closes with the words:

The inventive music shows the talent of Istvan Bastyai. The event was a resounding success.

And then, I pull out a heavy, A4 book and realise I'm holding the original script to the film. The film that became the first stepping stone towards a career in music in an exciting branch of the industry, still in its infancy. At the time of his lucky break, Stephen is thirty years old – not the typical age of a newcomer in the youth-obsessed music industry, particularly by today's standards, but then again there wasn't much about Stephen's life that was to be ordinary.

CHAPTER 4

Blissfully Blinkered

'Telegram for Istvan Holtzer.' The uniformed man hands Stephen an envelope and, with a quick nod, disappears back out into the square. Stephen stands in the doorway, staring down at the letter.

Up until this moment, it has been a day like most others, with Stephen at his desk listlessly shuffling papers, organising raw material receipts, while scheming and daydreaming.

Istvan – sending a wire as instructed – we need someone on piano for the new season – Could you come at once? Confirm if yes

Stephen knows he is going to take his friend up on the offer. He's less certain about how he's going to tell his parents. Immediately after his shift, he springs into action and, for the first time in his life, finds joy in bureaucratic detail – renewing his passport, applying for a work permit for Switzerland and packing. These are suddenly no longer tedious tasks, but necessary steps towards the next chapter of his life. Stephen doesn't miss a beat.

Aladar and Katica aren't exactly thrilled, but they accept his decision without any major falling-out or heartbreak (perhaps Stephen hadn't actually been that much of a help in the business and the thought of losing him as an employee wasn't totally unexpected or such a terrible prospect).

'You haven't got all that much money of your own to travel and live in Switzerland, Istvan,' Katica says, motherly worry etched upon her brow. 'How are you going to survive?'

'I have these!' Stephen holds up his hands in response. 'My hands are my money!' he exclaims in excited, self-assured tones.

Three days later, Stephen is on a train to Basel.

Of course, I thought I knew how to play the piano . . .

Stephen thumbs through the sheet music ahead of the trio's first performance, hoping that the pang of panic jolting through him isn't visible on his face. This, Stephen's first paid live performance as a professional musician, is well and truly a jump in at the deep end. The three of them, George, Paul and Stephen, are dressed in dinner jackets, about to go on stage and entertain the two hundred guests.

'You know our performance is being broadcast nationwide via radio, right, Istvan?' George smiles, testing his new piano player's nerves.

'Yeah, Paul here told me all about it.' Stephen smiles back, trying hard not to rise to the bait. Loosening his cravat, he follows the other two on to the stage, sits down at the piano, takes a deep breath and waits for Paul to count them in. The beat kicks in and the music flows. Where he can't follow the notation, Stephen relies on his ear and his intuition. The audience in the room, as well as those at home, leaning towards their radios, would never know that he isn't exactly playing what is on the page in front of him. Paul and George, on the other hand, do.

'Reading music has never been my strongest point,' Stephen says, mopping his brow, confessing to Paul, after receiving quite a harsh review by his bandmates after the show.

'Well, it better be your strong point by the next performance,' Paul replies.

Stephen doesn't mind that Paul is being strict. In fact, he's grateful to have someone pushing him to be technically better. The trio perform twice a day, once in the afternoon and then again in the evening. The repertoire is extensive and changes every two weeks with the arrival of a new guest singer. It's a gruelling schedule, a musical boot camp with Paul as self-appointed sergeant major. The real leader of the band, Stephen thinks, is George, whom he remembers as a *fabulous, versatile musician and a charming young man.*

Their evening performances are loud, fun and sometimes raucous, the atmosphere a hedonistic cocktail of carefree and youthful exuberance. The artists they accompany range from classical and cabaret singers to dancers and striptease artists. Each brings with them their own music for the band to learn and their own personality to dazzle the insatiable audiences. Still struggling to sight read, Stephen often spends the early hours of the morning learning new material off by heart to perform the next day. Occasionally during performances, Paul will step away from the drum kit and start playing the accordion, joining George up front as he solos on his violin. Whenever they play the tango, the crowd goes particularly wild. Stephen watches Paul, half in amusement, half in admiration, as he struts to the front of the stage and starts to tap dance on the podium, the accordion dangling from his neck. His showmanship lands the band rave reviews and Paul several dates.

Apart from this, Stephen refers to their drummer's eccentricities, *he was an excellent tutor and I learned a lot from him. He was a good-hearted man, trying to disguise this with rough talking.*

As the season and their three-month contract comes to an end, Stephen returns to Hungary an experienced performer. Following the success of the live nationwide broadcast, he is in demand both in Switzerland and back at home, picking up various contracts as a solo entertainer as well as with the trio.

As Hungarian citizens, Stephen and his fellow band members need to leave the country every nine months so as to not exceed their work permits. Those enforced breaks are not used for rest or leisure. Unlike his colleagues, Stephen performs wherever and whenever he can, building his audience in Budapest, as well as in Austria and Switzerland.

His address book is now bursting with creative, sequinned and cocktail-swilling contacts. Film producer Emil Martonffi is one of them. He hires Stephen to score the music for another romantic comedy. From the titles alone, *Temporarily Poor* and the aforementioned *Help, I Inherited!*, it seems class and social mobility must have been within the zeitgeist of the time.

I was firmly anchored in the theatrical world. I made a home for myself – and I was happy.

There's a page in one of Stephen's photo albums full of pictures of a woman called Roszi. Although I've never known much about her, everyone in my family knows her name. If I were to mention her to, say, my Aunt Julie, she'd nod in recognition and say something along the lines of, 'Yes, Roszi, my dad's true love.'

Roszi is undeniably beautiful. The photos are black-and-white, but from the contrast it's easy to make out that she has blonde hair. She wears it short and in waves, as per the fashion of the time. In one of the photos, a headshot, she's wearing a pill-box hat with a chic veil draped over her face. Through it, she stares directly into the lens. In Stephen's handwriting, the margin reads: 'Roszi: 1938–1940 a real

BIG LOVE OF MINE.' These capitalised words of longing would surely be hurtful to any woman who followed.

Stephen meets Roszi at the Anglo-Hungarian Society. She is what Stephen refers to as a 'starlet', a young actress, picking up small roles here and there at the Hunnia Film Studio. When he first sees her, she is dancing and Stephen remembers vividly how tightly his gaze was fixed upon her. His infatuation is immediate. He engages her in conversation that night and, very soon after, they are an item. For the first time, including his brief first marriage, Stephen feels genuinely in love.

I might have had love affairs in my student years, but this was the real thing.

Roszi is from a humble, working-class background – she has no formal education, and is new to Budapest's high-society arts scene. But she has what Stephen calls 'natural brains', and he describes her as 'good-natured, except when she lost her temper'. In that regard, they must have been a good match.

The relationship quickly becomes serious. Roszi moves out of her mother's home and into Stephen's bachelor pad in Buda. Katica grows very fond of Roszi – the two main women in Stephen's life spend a lot of time together, particularly when Stephen is away performing in Switzerland.

The love he feels for Roszi colours his surroundings. Stephen speaks amorously of Budapest, reflecting that: *Life was beautiful in the Pearl of the Danube.*

Budapest is still in bloom, boasting high culture – a smorgasbord of art, film and music. Stephen feels an energy pulsating through the city around the clock, from its late-night clubs and bars to its lunchtime restaurant hot spots and after-dinner drinks.

All this belonged to everyday life in Hungary, he remembers wistfully. In between his musical commitments in Switzerland, he and Roszi spend precious time together, absorbing all that Budapest has to offer.

There are a couple of pages in one of Stephen's photo albums that perfectly capture this time. They are full of small, square black-and-white group shots of Stephen and his friends leisurely sunbathing. There is something so timeless about these photographs, capturing the effortless cool of youth – the women sunbathing on the grass in fashionable swimwear and the men posing shirtless by the poolside. In Stephen's handwriting, the margins read: 'A bit of tennis playing and Palatinus Strand Budapest on the Margaret Island.'

There are rougher aspects of life in his hometown. The police in Budapest have a reputation for enforcing law and order with brutality. The 'not so polite police', as Stephen calls them, are more akin to military and are much feared.

If they took you in for some interrogation, Stephen says, *they'd first hit you over the head several times, then only ask you your name!*

There's a short pause on the tapes before he adds with a smirk: *But this, for hot-blooded Hungarians, I suppose was necessary.*

In March of 1938, Germany annexes Austria. Stephen mentions it only briefly, commenting on how willing the Austrian government and population were to join forces. The arrival of the Germans, he says, was *to the ecstasy of the Austrians.*

All the while, Hungary is passing a flurry of anti-Jewish legislation, mimicking race laws passed in Germany three years prior. Most importantly, a law was introduced that defined 'Jews' as a race, rather than a religion. Even if a person was fully assimilated or converted to a different religion, in the eyes of the law they would still be a Jew if, for instance, it could be proven that a person's grandparents were part of the Jewish community. Intermarriage between Jews and non-Jews was no longer permitted and Jews were excluded from certain professions, such as civil service roles. Professionals such as actors and musicians were still tolerated. And so, Stephen played on.

I seemed to be blissfully blinkered not to notice all this. My life did not change.

To Stephen and those within his circle, the laws passed by the Hungarian government are viewed as a simple act of diplomacy, small gestures to appease the Germans. It seems impossible, at this point, that Hungary would ever bend too far. Not for a second does Stephen think that Hungary would ever sell out its own people. Assured in his belief, he continues toing and froing between Switzerland and Hungary, working towards the life he always pictured for himself.

Some feel political temperatures rise, while others acclimatise to the gradual increase. With the burden of hindsight, it is impossible for me to cast an impartial eye on my grandfather's story. I look at the carefree faces sunbathing by the pool and feel my heart break. I want to shout at them all, through time and the fading ink: 'Get out of the water, it's getting too hot.'

But even with awareness of a growing threat, how bad does it have to be before we uproot, take all our belongings and our loved ones by the hand to leave all we know behind?

By the summer of 1938, some Hungarian Jews are doing just that. Among them are Istvan Székely and Irene Agay. They plan to move to America and they extend an invitation to Stephen.

'I have all the rights to show the film internationally, you see,' his namesake tells Stephen over a strong, black coffee.

'We're going to tour the film, performing in all the towns where Hungarian immigrants have settled – Washington, Denver, through to California. It's a growing market,' he adds, the darker implications of this not lost on Stephen.

'Look, I want to hold speeches after the film . . . Irene is going to sing and dance. You should come with us and play the music, come play the piano!'

Some people say that I was crazy not to go with them, that it was an opportunity of a lifetime. They said it was because I did not want to leave Roszi. There was an element of truth in this, but somehow I felt it may have been irrevocably too far from my parents, whom I adored – that was my main motive. Well . . . I did not go to America.

Instead of Stephen, Istvan and Irene invite one of their junior staff writers to join them: *Someone who helped with the scripts and made tea*, Stephen laughs. For a moment, I'm unsure whether there's a hint of resentment in his voice. I think there might be, but I feel it's directed not at the man who went in his stead and more towards his own misfortune in this path untaken.

You know, it turns out that he went on to marry Veronica Lake, Stephen shares, his voice now lighter with that animated bounce I'm growing used to. *So really, I could have married Veronica Lake.*

Somewhere amid this whirlwind of musical activity, Stephen is introduced to Alvia Suli, an American singer with Hungarian roots. In Budapest to visit family, she meets Stephen through his film producer friends. In his tapes, he describes her as a 'famous diseuse', which prompts me to pause his retelling and look up the term. It's often used to refer to a female artist who recites poetry or other texts set to music. Stephen goes on to say that *she didn't have the distance*

– meaning she didn't have a wide vocal range – *but she had a lot of charm.*

Stephen and Alvia decide to collaborate and he proceeds to arrange music to suit her range. They land a contract with a large restaurant called The Dunacorzo along the Danube River where, together with a drummer, they perform to a sold-out audience of four hundred every night. This is by far the biggest performance contract Stephen has won in his native Hungary. I have photographs of these performances and they radiate. A close-up of the stage shows Alvia, in a silver sequinned gown with flowing mid-length sleeves, standing in front of the piano. Her arms are outstretched, reaching behind her in mid-movement. Her head is tilted to one side and she's smiling with a warm, doe-eyed face, framed by a wavy bob adorned with a matching sequinned headdress. Stephen is wearing a suit, crisp white shirt and a bow tie. He's sitting at the piano behind Alvia and is looking straight into the camera with that same serene hint of a smile that I recognise from other photographs of him play-ing piano. Examining the photo more closely, I see a small table to the side of the stage, covered with what looks like whisky glasses. In this moment, I remember a story my dad once told me. So many audience members wanted to buy Stephen drinks as a token of appreciation, he couldn't possibly have drunk them all and still been able to play. So, the story goes that he struck a deal with the barman: audiences would order a drink for Stephen and the barman knew to fill the glass with water or juice instead of alcohol. At the end of the night, Stephen and the barman would split the money accrued by this little scheme. Smiling at the memory (I believe my dad divulged this story when he saw that audience members were offering to buy me whisky shots at my shows and perhaps wanted to steer me in a different direction), I conclude that the glasses on that little table are most likely filled with water.

At The Dunacorzo, Katica and Aladar come to see Stephen perform in public for the first time. Together with his siblings, they take a seat at a table close to the stage area. His parents are taken aback by just how popular their son seems to be. When the audience jump to their feet to give Stephen a standing ovation, as he gets up from the piano to take a bow next to Alvia at the end of the performance, Katica and Aladar beam at one another with parental pride.

Once their first contract runs out, Stephen returns to Switzerland. This time, with a different trio and for an even more prestigious gig. Their contract is with the Lausanne Palace Hotel, a five-star hotel which Stephen says is home to, among others, the exiled King of Spain. This gig, though prestigious, is not nearly as much fun as his prior engagements. Stephen recalls the subdued, very formal atmosphere, the music serving as a soft and inoffensive backdrop to the gentries' dining experience. Occasionally, there is some polite, after-dinner dancing to the jazz numbers Stephen and his band play later in the evening. Reflecting on this engagement, Stephen shares that: *The violin was the most important instrument – the piano had no great role here*, and therefore concludes: *I did not enjoy it very much . . . but I enjoyed Lausanne!*

The season comes to a close and Stephen decides to stay. In Switzerland, solo piano entertainers are a rarity and, with his repertoire now consisting of everything from Beethoven to various pop and folk songs, operettas, as well as his own compositions, Stephen is in a position where he can pick and choose among the many contracts he's offered. He signs as a solo performer with Hotel De La

Paix, which offers beautiful views of Lake Geneva and the Alps from its ornate balconies.

Stephen shares that the key to finding success as a solo performer is having a vast repertoire to call upon and the ability to read and cater to the energy of a room. In his opinion, this is just as important, if not more so, than the actual quality of piano playing – a technically perfect performance can become dull if the performer isn't connecting with the audience.

I love listening to Stephen reminisce about his set at Hotel De La Paix – he talks about playing Chopin, Bach, Mozart, Schubert and Tchaikovsky, as well as overtures and songs from popular operettas and musical theatre pieces of the day. Stephen stresses the importance of having an extensive knowledge of jazz, and mentions performing pieces by Gershwin and Cole Porter. Catering to the international crowd, he learns and performs folk songs and national anthems from across Europe and includes older tunes from as far back as 1902, *for the older folks.*

All this was necessary to make a name for yourself and also to make money.

In the afternoons, Stephen is free to roam around Lausanne. He cherishes these moments as a solo traveller, taking in all the local food, entertainment and beautiful scenery. On one such afternoon, Stephen feels content, albeit slightly hungover, as he walks past a dance hall. Seeking refuge from the August sun beating down on the pristine pavement, he decides to take a drink and see what the establishment is like.

As he steps inside, he's somewhat taken aback by the raucous atmosphere. There's a big band playing, people dancing and a group of excited young women grouped together at the front of the stage.

He follows their gaze and soon realises what the excitement is all about. There, tap dancing on the podium with an accordion swinging around his neck, is Paul. With a wide smile, Stephen takes a seat at the bar and watches his friend do his thing.

At the end of his set, Paul rushes towards the bar. Upon spying Stephen, he dramatically clutches his heart in disbelief. Stephen jumps up from his seat and they fall into a tight embrace.

'My friend!' Paul draws out the word in excitement. 'I haven't seen you in . . . how long has it been . . . over a year now?'

'I know, time flies when you're tap dancing!' Stephen laughs.

'The band sound great, by the way,' Stephen acknowledges, pointing towards the empty stage as the barman hands Paul a drink on the house.

'So, have you been in Switzerland this whole time?' Stephen asks.

'Yes, actually!' Paul replies, wide-eyed. 'The band is a Swiss band . . . Istvan, it's great: I am exempt from all restrictions! Mr Cole, the band leader, simply said to the authorities that he needs me and that there's no one else like me to be found in Switzerland . . . and that was that!'

'There is no one quite like you in Hungary, either!' Stephen teases before congratulating him on his success. No matter how genuine the well wishes, there is always an element of competition among peers. Stephen can't help but feel a pang of jealousy. For a fleeting moment he thinks that he, too, would be worthy of such special status. Changing the subject, Stephen takes a sip from his glass and then turns to Paul: 'How's George? Have you heard from him?'

'Yes – I – have,' Paul shouts, dramatically punctuating each word with a knock of his glass on the wooden bar, indicating that good gossip is underway.

'George went to America! You know he has a little son, right? He's only about five years old now, but guess what? He plays the drums! He plays them really well! And get this, Istvan – they perform together in variety shows; I think they're doing really well out of it.'

Stephen raises his eyebrows in disbelief, before breaking into laughter as the friends start to reminisce about their time on stage together. It isn't until Stephen realises the time and says that he needs to get back to the hotel for his evening performance, that Paul realises he has yet to ask what Stephen is doing at the moment.

As Stephen tells him that he is employed as a solo artist, his friend is quick to interrupt him: 'Solo? You can't play solo, Istvan; you know you need a really big repertoire for that.'

'I have a big repertoire,' Stephen replies with a slight exasperation.

'Not big enough!' Paul shouts comically, punching the air. 'Come on, follow me – I have loads of sheet music that you can have.'

Stephen decides to humour his friend, following him backstage.

From a far corner of the room, Paul heaves out a large suitcase full of sheet music and drops it on the floor in front of Stephen. 'Here! This should be enough . . . You can have this, I don't need them any more.' He smiles. Stephen knows that, regardless of whether or not he actually needs this amount of music, he has no option other than to accept Paul's offer.

He got me a big suitcase full of sheet music. I could barely carry it. Good old Paul . . . I could only use a small fraction of it.

Stephen and Paul eventually lose track of one another. Mr Cole's big band moves on and Paul with it.

As I learn this story about Paul and his big band, I remember the box full of sheet music in my dad's attic. I smile as I realise that this must be where they came from. The more I tune into Stephen's past, the more my own sense of self seems to shift. I grew up with his piano, among all these wonderfully well-travelled treasures, having no idea how much history they held. I was so unaware of their presence, but now every piece of sheet music and every photograph springs to life and glitters with significance.

I'm retracing Stephen's steps, at least virtually. To my surprise, both the Lausanne Palace Hotel and the Hotel De La Paix still exist and are operating as rather high-end-looking five- and four-star resorts. I'm on Hotel De La Paix's website looking at photographs of the rooms. I see the view from the balcony and let out a small but audible gasp. I've seen this view before. I reach for one of Stephen's photo albums and carefully thumb through the pages. In one particular photo, Stephen is resting against the balcony railing, one arm bent at an angle, one arm outstretched. His head is tilted to the right and he's smiling, his eyes squinting slightly in the sun. I carefully remove the photo from the album and turn it over. In his handwriting, it reads: 'Lausanne, 1938.'

I am Stephen de Bastion, a laboured voice stumbles uncomfortably. I'm just testing this tape recorder because, unfortunately, ten years ago my voice was much more powerful than it is now. Before I go further in this story of mine, I'd like to find out whether it's any good to talk into this microphone!

This is how the cassette labelled 'Stephen tells his war story – Part 1' begins. Stephen's voice breaks into a weak but charming laugh at the end of that first sentence. On the last word, he places all the emphasis on the first syllable, drawing out the 'i' in 'microphone'. I listen to him grab the cassette recorder and pull it towards him across what sounds like a weathered wooden tabletop. There's the click of the pause button, a fraction of silence, followed by a second click, before he concludes with a noticeable lift in his voice: *This tape seems to be quite good!*

I'm going to concentrate to speak during the years of the war and what happened to me during the years of 1939 and 1944.

But he didn't. Although my grandfather had sat down to record his war story, he couldn't help but tell his story first, a story I recognise all too well. It's uncanny how much of my dad and myself I find mirrored in Stephen's drive and passion for music. I also hear my father in Stephen's deliberate speech (although his words are coated with a thick Hungarian accent while my dad spoke with a classic BBC Radio 4 kind of voice) and in the quiet authority and the warmth of his speech.

My heart fills with thoughts of beauty and sadness in equal measure as I learn just how much Stephen and I would have to share. As working musicians, we have lived such similar experiences, eighty years apart. If only we could talk over a glass of wine around the piano.

CHAPTER 5

In Splendid Isolation

*I*t must have been around August, Roszi came to see me.

In the cassette tapes, Roszi gets only a fleeting mention, but in one of the handwritten letters, Stephen shares their story. It is a tale of heartbreak for both and will be one of the only decisions Stephen truly comes to regret. Roszi is pregnant and Stephen's response is not the one she perhaps expects or at least hopes for.

It was difficult for both of us, Stephen writes nearly half a century later, *for her to persuade me, for me to decide whether to listen to my feelings to keep her and the child or listen to my reason and not marry her.*

If he chooses marriage, Stephen fears, it will jeopardise his work permit in Switzerland, where he is earning good money and building a steady reputation. He does not want to give that up. He also shares concern about bringing a child into a world teetering at the precipice of war. The more honest reasons Stephen gives for not wanting a family are more personal.

My last marriage must have still left some scars, and somehow I did not feel I would be capable to look after a family, he admits. At this juncture in his life, Stephen is simply not willing to give up the independence he had worked so hard to obtain. He's now earning money as a professional piano player both at home and abroad, and fears that becoming a father will severely limit his opportunities.

He concludes: *In normal circumstances, perhaps it would have been possible, but after a long deliberation, I decided to stay and not to marry Roszi.*

Stephen starts to feel remorse, an unfamiliar sensation of heaviness in the pit of his stomach, as soon as they part ways at the train station in Zürich. They leave things open-ended, but in their hearts, they both know that their love affair has come to an end and will most likely not be reparable. It must have been a difficult journey home for Roszi, heartbroken and bearing the burden of their relationship, alone.

Through my twenty-first-century lens, I cannot help but feel protective over Roszi and see her as vulnerable in this relationship. She is a young girl, in love with a man twelve years her senior. For Stephen, it will be easy to slip back into his routine and continue with his life, no matter how real and deep the pain is that he feels when their love affair comes to an end. Stephen choosing himself, choosing independence, has serious consequences for Roszi. For her, it is a lose-lose situation – at this point, abortion is still illegal in Hungary, but equally, raising a child as a single mother out of wedlock is not an option afforded to her by society. Regardless of whether nineteen-year-old Roszi may have wanted the child or not, she sees no option other than to abort the pregnancy illegally. Stephen later learns that Roszi undergoes a risky, late abortion, resulting in her hospitalisation for weeks.

On the first of September, the war was declared and we decided she will go back and see what the future will bring us. Her going back is the end of a beautiful love affair.

While Stephen is nursing a broken heart, Switzerland prepares for an invasion that will never come. Within days, thousands of troops are mobilised, but Germany does not attack and Switzerland remains independent. Stephen's elected home remains neutral, which allows him to continue life without giving much thought to the world's turmoil. Besides, he is still far too preoccupied with his own feelings of unrest.

As the month of September comes to a close, it is time for Stephen to find employment for the winter season. Through a friend, he hears of a vacancy at Hotel Central in the picturesque Alpine village of Villars-sur-Ollon and is given the telephone number of the proprietor, Mr Favor. On the phone, Mr Favor is curt, unwilling to give much time or information to Stephen. He confirms that they are looking for a pianist to cover the winter season. When Stephen asks what the salary is, Mr Favor simply says: 'Come up and see me – show me what you can do and then we'll talk.'

It is already dark when Stephen arrives late in the afternoon on the agreed date. The traditional alpine-style hotel is nestled on the mountainside. Against the night sky, the peaks on the far side of the valley are a dark silhouette. Stephen climbs up the steps, opens the door and walks up to reception. The walls and ceilings are lined with light wooden panelling that match the thick, ornately carved wooden chairs, tables and benches. The restaurant on the ground floor is a beautiful brasserie, featuring a round stone fireplace in the middle of the room. Here, Stephen is told by the receptionist, Mr Favor prepares the fondue dishes himself. Stephen is asked to wait until the proprietor is ready to see him, so he takes a seat on one of the many, heavy wooden benches. During Stephen's lengthy wait, Mr Favor pops his head into the room several times to apologise, to say how busy he is in the restaurant, and to ask Stephen to wait a little longer. A gigging musician will encounter many a strange situation. Stephen begins to feel that this might be one of those nights – full of surreal and beautiful circumstances. He smiles to himself as he can't help but notice how well the proprietor's appearance matches the voice he heard on the phone – Mr Favor is a big, burly man. His shirtsleeves are rolled up past his elbows and his apron is covered in flour.

When he finally comes out to greet Stephen properly, it is almost 10 p.m. He leads Stephen through the restaurant and into a darkened room. Usually one to keep his cool and his cards close to his chest, Stephen is in awe of the scene. There is an undeniable tranquillity and beauty surrounding him. The wood-panelled room boasts large, rectangular windows looking out onto the Alps. With wide-eyed reverence, Stephen sees the snow-capped peaks shimmering majestically in the night, illuminated by a bright, full moon. The guests, who are sat around wooden tables enjoying their post-dinner drinks, seem equally transfixed by the view.

'Here is the piano.' Mr Favor's raspy voice pulls Stephen back into the moment.

I heard his voice behind me. The room was silent. I sat down and was under such a spell.

Stephen sits at the piano. He looks out into the room and sees a fleet of floating candlelight, shards of yellow floating on top of a dark sea of tables. In this moment, he feels a sense of peace he hasn't experienced since he parted ways with Roszi; this is exactly where he is supposed to be. Musical adventures such as this – the beauty of the surroundings, the anticipation of performance, the feeling that, tonight, anything could happen – are Stephen's calling. This is the life he wants.

As he starts to play, he feels as though he is in a trance and not in control of his fingers moving across the keys. Some performances are magical. It is the sum of so many parts – the performer's state of mind, the audience's receptiveness, the setting, the sound – when they all come together, we experience music at its best: a true, spiritual connection. The room comes alive and Stephen feels as though his playing is setting the surroundings alight. It is as though a current rushes through him and the audience, as they jump up to dance. A barman appears next to Stephen and asks him what he would like to drink. He promptly returns with the finest whisky on offer.

I played and played. The people, it was full, danced and clapped.

Stephen lets himself fall into the night. The energy lasts well into the early hours until finally, at four in the morning, he climbs up the staircase and into his room after the last of the guests have danced their final dance.

The next morning, Stephen feels happy. It strikes him as slightly strange though that he appears to still be on some sort of audition at the hotel, but when Mr Favor asks him to play for an hour at teatime, Stephen agrees. After his set, a well-dressed businessman approaches Stephen at the piano and leans over to ask: 'How long will you be playing here for?'

'You'll have to ask Mr Favor!' Stephen laughs. 'He hasn't offered me a contract yet.'

The man places a generous tip on top of the piano and mumbles something along the lines of: 'I hope you stay for a long while,' before shuffling out of the room.

Over the next few days, Stephen stays at Hotel Central, performing and assuming an implied contract of sorts. He sees Mr Favor only fleetingly. He is usually in a rush, carrying pots of bubbling, melted cheese. Determined to pin him down, Stephen decides to confront Mr Favor in his office. They narrowly miss a collision in the hallway, as Mr Favor steps out of his room just as Stephen is bursting in.

'Mr Favor.' Stephen straightens out his shirt as he speaks. 'What about my contract?'

With a slight air of annoyance, but a calm and collected voice, Mr Favor points behind Stephen and says: 'Go to my office and tell my secretary your terms. She'll write them out and I'll sign it. I'd like you to stay until the end of April, please.'

Stephen does not exploit Mr Favor's trust and requests a reasonable salary. He does, however, add an unusual stipulation in his contract. Stephen requests that there be no curfew, that he can play for as long as he wishes – throughout the whole night, if he so pleases.

I was in splendid isolation. The war did not exist up in the mountains.

In these winter months, Stephen plays a flowery song of denial. He bathes in the beauty of his surroundings and in the carelessness of the tourists enjoying their ski holidays. He indulges in his popularity up in the mountains. Often guests invite him to their chalets after hours, where the party and Stephen's performance go on past sunrise. In the afternoons, Stephen is taken out for lunch or drinks, and enjoys fleeting affairs, all in between his feverish sets at Hotel Central. On top of his fee, the guests tip him generously, particularly in the small hours of the night. *I never left the mountain*, Stephen writes, *so I was saving a lot.*

There's testimony of these parties and Stephen's popularity in his photo albums. One of them contains six pages dedicated to this time. Many of the black-and-white photos are group shots and snap-shots of young men and women posing in front of snowy mountain peaks. Stephen's handwritten caption in the margins reads: 'Me and Friends, lots of them.' One photograph is a portrait of a strikingly beautiful woman, resting her head delicately on her knuckles and directing her gaze downward. I carefully lift it off the page and turn it around to see if there are any clues as to who she might be. It simply reads: 'One of my fans.'

My favourites of these photographs are two larger photos of the chalets themselves. Across the white walls, above the wicker armchairs and wooden bar, are bits of scores from Stephen's compositions, painted on by the holidaying guests surrounded by little decorative musical notes. Stephen's music making a literal mark.

In early spring, Stephen indulges in occasional chauffeured day trips down to Lausanne, where he enjoys restaurant and spa visits. After a day of leisure, the car would take him back up the mountain in time for his evening performance at the hotel.

April comes, bringing his engagement at Hotel Central to an end. Before Stephen leaves the mountain, Mr Favor offers him a contract for the next winter season. Stephen accepts and returns to a small, rented flat in Lausanne with a diary full of performance commitments that would see him through the next twelve months. Under the spell of the Alps, he has lost track of time. He realises that he has now been in Switzerland for eleven months and his work permit's expiry is imminent.

The authorities, perhaps increasingly busied by the bureaucracy of conflict, do not bend the rules for Stephen and his plea to extend his permit is denied. This is much to his chagrin. Stephen is on a roll and does not want to stop performing. If he leaves Switzerland for too long, he fears that precious career momentum might be lost and so he continues to try to convince the authorities to make an exception. Polite persistence pays off at least in part. They finally agree to shorten the time of exile – allowing him to return to Switzerland after just one month's break instead of the usual three. Deeming this too short a time to head back to Hungary for more shows, Stephen takes a break for the first time since he embarked on this relentless journey of performing. He's saved up plenty of money and decides to treat himself: he will go on holiday instead of going home to Budapest. In a moment of carefree whim, Stephen walks into a travel bureau and asks for holiday deals.

'Where are you looking to holiday, sir?' the uniformed woman behind the counter asks.

Never missing a performance opportunity, Stephen smiles and raises his eyebrows in playful suspense.

'Just one moment, please.' He closes his eyes and hovers with his index finger over the map of Europe laid out underneath glass on top of the desk between him and the travel agent. He lets his hand drop at random and opens his eyes to see where his finger had landed.

'Rapallo – I'd like to go to Italy, please.'

Rapallo was deserted – it was war and there were no tourists.

Stephen is staying in a hotel on the Italian Riviera. He is content with his room, which overlooks the sea. He rents an upright piano on which he composes feverishly, willing the time to pass and his picturesque exile to come to an end.

The Italian coastal town is eerily quiet. There are some tourists left – there aren't many who still feel carefree enough to holiday in the current political climate – but on his walks, Stephen finds it hard to tell who of the passers-by are genuine tourists and who are secret police. *It didn't bother me . . . or better said,* he corrects himself, *they did not bother me.*

He spends his days swimming, exploring deserted, cobblestoned streets and taking in the sights. In the evenings, he indulges in plenty of local red wine, which often leads to summer flirtations with the few remaining holidaymakers. But the lightness in the air does not linger. Italy, an ally of Germany in war, is devaluing foreign currency at will. The Swiss francs Stephen is carrying are becoming less valuable by the day and he is forced to dig deeper into his savings in order to afford his stay.

One evening Stephen is sitting outside the hotel grounds, reclining on what he calls a 'Liegestuhl', the German word for sunlounger. His shirt is unbuttoned and his sleeves are rolled up, the heat of the afternoon sun still hanging in the night sky. A woman exits from the lobby and walks towards Stephen. The previous night they had shared a bottle of wine and friendly, frivolous chat in the hotel bar. In silence, she sits on the chair next to him and directs her gaze up towards the starry sky. She's wearing a long, silk dressing gown that's draped elegantly over a swimming costume. Her demeanour is stonier than it was last night and Stephen finds her expression hard to read. Eventually, noticing his gaze, she turns to him and breaks the silence: 'Have you heard that Hitler invaded Belgium?'

Stephen calls home the following morning. Overnight, Italy had closed its borders to Switzerland. His mother urges him to travel to Genoa, to take a boat to America. But Katica knows her son. She knows his stubborn nature and that, as much as he loves his musical adventures and independence, he would never leave his mother behind. Stephen refuses to take her advice and travels back to Hungary, back to his family.

CHAPTER 6

The Family Tree

My dad always said that Katica and the piano belonged together. No matter where in the house the piano stood – my mother constantly rearranged the furniture and redecorated – Katica's portrait always hung so that she peered over her shoulder, down at her Blüthner baby grand.

I'm embarrassed at how old I was when I realised that family trees are patriarchal, the women appearing out of thin air and tied to no one, save for the men they marry. Shortly after the turn of the century, Katica Schwartz became Katica Holtzer and the piano became part of our family.

Up until marriage, Katica's life was painted in an illusion of independence. She grew up as one of six in Kecskemét, a midsized town situated halfway between Budapest and Szeged. My great-grandmother was an incredibly gifted student and the first Jewish girl to take exams at a boys' grammar school. At this time, there were already legal limitations on how many Jewish students were able to access higher education. For Jewish girls, this was an even less common achievement. She did well academically, but just like her son, her real passion and talent lay in the arts. She was the first serious pianist in the family and came alive when expressing her creativity, be it playing music, painting or writing poetry. Her father, Gustav Schwartz, allowed her to go to university. She studied arts in

Budapest and was a student of Hungarian literary historian Zsolt Beöthy. During those studies, she travelled to Italy to paint. Two paintings from that time are framed and hang among the family portraits in our home in Berlin. My favourite is a vertical landscape of what looks like the city walls of an Italian town. The paint is applied richly, the shading of the earthy browns perfectly illustrates the sunlight bouncing off the tower in the centre of the painting. There's something slightly off about the perspective, but the two tiny figures depicted in the entrance of the tower are so sweet and delicate, at least my untrained eye would never have guessed that this was the work of a student. I grew up totally unaware that this painting was hers. That's not to say that nobody told me, I'm sure at some point someone did, but up until I committed to writing this book, I've had a strange weakness to retain information pertaining to my family tree, the weight of its branches somehow rendering my memory for names and details useless. No matter how many times I was shown a family tree, I would often point at one of the portraits I grew up with and ask my dad, 'So who's that again?' or stare at a name and say, 'So how are they related to us?'

While it was still highly unusual for women to attend university, I imagine Katica's father would have deemed the arts an acceptable subject for a lady of certain social stature. The 'certain social stature' was new for the Schwartz family, who had only recently climbed up the social ladder from humble agricultural beginnings. As much as Katica excelled in her studies, she did not complete her course and dropped out when Aladar proposed marriage.

I realise now that I only know my Great-grandmother Katica through the lens of the men in her life. Her father, husband and son, who clearly loved her dearly. In their stories, she is portrayed as a confident, outspoken, intelligent and talented woman. She is at least awarded adjectives that go beyond her physical attributes, which is not something that can be said for most women in my grandfather's retelling. I'll never truly know how she felt about all of this at the time, how she felt about not finishing her studies, about giving up her home to move to Szeged after the wedding, about not pursuing her own interests.

According to Stephen, Katica never stopped talking passionately about Firenze and Rome.

Her husband Aladar was an extremely gentle, soft-spoken and kind man. I can see this behind his rosy cheeks and sparkly brown eyes in his portrait. This sensitivity would lead him to choose a particularly thoughtful engagement present for his wife-to-be, something he knew his independent, art- and music-loving partner would adore. Something of significance.

As for Aladar and Katica's relationship, photographs and passed-down stories point towards a contented companionship, even if it may not have been a passionate love. Divorce and second marriages were actually not uncommon on either side of the family tree, but my great-grandparents stayed together until the end.

This could be the story of Katica the piano player. But I have no recordings of her playing. To my knowledge, she never performed in public. If she composed her own songs, which in my heart I feel she must have, they are lost in time. This could also be the story of Annie the piano player, Katica's only daughter, who was equally gifted in the arts and loved playing the piano and writing poetry as much as she enjoyed singing. Just as her mother had done, Annie followed the path dictated by social norms around her gender. She never pursued music professionally and married early, a man nearly twice her age, for security. And so this is not Katica's story, nor Annie's, but that of the firstborn son. He may not have been given absolute freedom to pursue music as a career, but due to being born a man, he was able to take it.

The world into which Stephen and his siblings were born, the one Katica became a part of in marriage, is so alien to me, it feels a fiction. When I think of the family name as it was in its glory days, the royal Bastyai Holtzer, my mind fills with fantastical images of opulence, a sort of Rolodex of fine textiles, beautifully crafted furniture, Persian rugs, apartments with high ceilings filled with antiques, those family portraits and our piano. The Holtzer family even has its own coat of arms. We have it framed in the doorway in my parents' home in Berlin – three bastions in formation on the shield and a golden lion yielding a sword on top of a crown. The colours of the wreaths are red and blue.

It's a strange sensation to see your family's personal history slot so neatly into a textbook on the Holocaust. To give further context to Stephen's story, of his journey, and of those who came before him, I buy a book with the grim title *Politics of Genocide: The Holocaust in Hungary*, by Randolph L. Braham. I'm reading it while I'm on tour, travelling across the UK by trains. In my breaks from reading, the book rests on the little table in front of my seat next to a half-empty take-away coffee cup, and I watch its ominous reflection in the window overlaying the otherwise peaceful, rolling hills of Middle England.

The Holtzer family tree has deep roots. Its branches are intertwined with the history of the town of Szeged and can be traced as far back as the second half of the eighteenth century. The story of the rise and fall of S. Holtzer & Sons starts with Jakab Holtzer. I have no physical description of him, but the family have dark hair, delicate facial features and a small frame. Jakab is believed to be the first Hungarian family member. He moved to Szeged from modern-day Czech Republic during an early wave of immigration in the seventeen hundreds.

It's likely that the reason why Jakab migrated to Szeged in the first place was to escape pogroms, antisemitic massacres and assaults in the region, which took place throughout the eighteenth and nineteenth centuries in Eastern and Central Europe. Antisemitism has been present in public discourse and political life for centuries.

In his newly elected home, Jakab sold fabrics as an independent street merchant. He and his wife were one of only eleven Jewish families who were granted official permission to settle. They led a modest life and went on to have four children, two sons and two daughters. It was the eldest son, Salamon, who founded the S. Holtzer & Sons company in 1848 and that date is no coincidence. In 1848 it became legal for people who belonged to the Jewish faith to own businesses in Hungary. Before that, they were prohibited from doing so.

Assisted by his father's knowledge of fabrics, Salamon started trading from their home. Within a decade, the company had grown significantly. But while the Holtzer family and business prospered in Szeged, larger things were at play on the world stage. In the very same year of 1848, thousands of civilians participated in antisemitic attacks in over thirty cities across Hungary as a backlash to the liberties granted. Meanwhile, tensions were rising across Continental Europe, between an old feudal and a new parliamentary system. In a gust of change, Hungary became the third country in Europe to introduce new laws favouring a more progressive democratic government. When the Emperor of Austria and King of Hungary, Franz Joseph I, revoked those laws in a hubristic attempt to squash the movement, the conflict escalated. Military intervention in the Kingdom of Hungary resulted in a strong nationalistic push and the outbreak of the Hungarian War of Independence.

Around 40 per cent of soldiers in the Hungarian Revolutionary Army consisted of ethnic minorities; Salamon Holtzer was one of them. He felt immense pride in his native and his parents' elected home. While his parents spoke and corresponded mostly in German and Yiddish, Salamon assimilated and saw himself primarily as Hungarian. He still played an active role in the religious community, but advocated for modernisation within it. And so, during Hungary's War of Independence, Salamon fought for his country as a volunteer soldier. However, after a year of fighting, the mighty joint army of Russia and Austria eventually defeated the Hungarian forces and Hungary was once again under the rule of the crown.

When Salamon returned home, he found S. Holtzer & Sons was flourishing. In his absence, his wife Francisca had run the business, as well as looking after their five children.

Salamon died peacefully in his home in 1886 at the age of seventy-five. The company lived on, with Salamon's eldest son, Jakob (named after his grandfather), taking over and turning the cottage industry into an empire.

Jakob Holtzer was an extraordinarily hard-working individual. He lived a frugal life – everything he earned was either reinvested into the company and put towards growing a future for his children or put back into the community. Family lore has it he'd sew his trouser's and jacket pockets shut, so that he wouldn't carry money with him and wouldn't be tempted to spend it on anything he deemed frivolous. Whatever profit was left at the end of a tax year, he'd invest in real estate, opening several branches of the business across Hungary and further afield in modern-day Serbia and Romania, and eventually buying tenement buildings in Szeged, Budapest and Berlin.

This third-generation immigrant, whose grandfather came to Hungary as a street merchant, propelled the family into the upper middle class. Jakob expanded the company to include a retail branch with ready-to-wear men's clothing as well as a tailoring salon where uniforms and suits were made to measure. They also started stocking various lining fabrics and haberdashery, as well as hats, buttons and trimmings. The company now had international wholesale clients in places such as London and Vienna, and were commissioned by the Hungarian royal family to create ceremonial costumes for the King's visit to Szeged. Their flagship shop stood in today's Deak Ferenc Street in Szeged. Jakob bought the entire residential building, with the shop flourishing on the ground floor and spilling out into the courtyard.

In the Holtzer family, jokes have generational longevity. The majority of anecdotes about my ancestors consist of their witticisms and wisecracking. As serious as Jakob was about the business, he was known for his jovial nature. My Aunt Julie remembers a passed-down story of how Jakob, a rather large man, would sit, stomach protruding, gesturing with his cane towards the door of his top-floor apartment, jokingly ordering the horse and cart to come and pick him up from the couch.

Jakob was an exceptional individual and he found his equal in his wife, Julia Gruber. A confident, highly educated woman with a strong sense of self and community, Julia dedicated her life to charity, which was equally as important in the ascent of the Holtzer family as the actual textile business itself. From 1867 onwards, she was an active board member of one of the biggest charitable organisations, the Women's Society, and was later voted president. In this role, she lobbied for and oversaw countless charitable projects, such as the construction of an orphanage and an almshouse. Together with her husband and brother-in-law, she even set up a scholarship for children to attend university. S. Holtzer & Sons would also provide clothing for free to local families in need.

Julia and Jakob had six children, three sons and three daughters. The sons, Tivador, Emil and my great-grandfather, Aladar, were each given an equal stake in the company, making them the fourth generation in the family to work in textiles in Szeged. The sons also became proprietors of the family's real estate. The daughters were not given any share of the business or property, but were 'financially taken care of'.

Julia loved and had a great knowledge of the arts. She was part of Szeged's Art Lovers Society, who have it documented that she was an avid collector of paintings, Meissen and Zsolnay porcelain, Murano glassware, Brussels lace and antiques . . . all the finer things. Besides collecting, it was Julia who commissioned portraits of family members. She employed her favourite artists, among them Odon Heller and Sandor Nyilasy, to capture the Holtzer family in oil paints.

Julia and Jakob's portraits are among those in our home and, apart from Katica's grand oil painting, they are my favourites. Julia looks like royalty. Her light brown curly hair is in a stylish up-do and is adorned with what look like tiny pearl daisies. She's wearing the most spectacular light blue jacket with puff sleeves and large, beautifully embroidered lapels that match the cream, ruffle-collared blouse underneath. Jakob, true to character, is wearing much simpler clothes – a black smock, black cravat and a white cotton shirt. He is sporting one of those upward curled moustaches. It's tinted grey, as is his short, otherwise dark-brown hair. In their frames, Jakob is looking to the left and Julia to the right, so that, if hung correctly, they're looking towards one another.

The Holtzer family contributed so much to the city of Szeged (alongside their charity work they are credited with founding the local football team and financing Szeged's first riverbank public beach) that they were bestowed an honorary title of nobility by the Hungarian royal family. The very same monarch that his father had gone to war against was now honouring his family's achievements, fully accepting them as Hungarian, as valuable members of society. The family would joke for generations that the royal family gave out the title to get away with not paying for textiles.

Jakob Holtzer died in 1906. Julia led the firm for a couple of years before eventually handing it over to her sons. She got to know her grandchildren. She got to commission that oil painting of little Stephen, sitting impatiently in that wicker chair on the balcony of Julia's apartment. I imagine Katica would have got on well with her mother-in-law, sharing a passion for art and both being outspoken, independent women.

Researching the history of S. Holtzer & Sons has been made so easy for me. Just as I embark on the journey of writing this book, I learn that a synagogue in Szeged is including the Holtzer family in a new exhibition on families of note to the town. It's as if Stephen is magically conducting me, guiding me through the symphony of his life with ease. Reading the exhibition booklet, I learn that the company officially folded in 1948, exactly one hundred years after its inception. The booklet is a dark blue A5 pamphlet, including scanned photographs and documents. The text is in Hungarian, with a rough English translation. One sentence with regard to the last days of the company is particularly jarring to me: 'In 1945 Emil Holtzer died of starvation in the poor house.' Life, for the Holtzer family, must have taken a dark turn.

Like a stencil, my family story continues to fit neatly on to the evolution of antisemitism in Hungary. Perhaps one of the reasons why Aladar was so adamant that Stephen attend university was that exactly as he was due to go, new anti-Jewish laws restricted the percentage of Jewish students to 6 per cent (the supposed equivalent to the overall percentage of Jewish Hungarians; in reality, it was 5 per cent). Incidentally, Hungary was the first European country to pass such a law in the twentieth century, ahead of Germany. Despite this and the growing racist propaganda, as well as mounting pressure from Nazi Germany, liberal, established families such as mine felt safe. They clung to a conviction that their country would not betray them. No matter how little Aladar, Katica and their children related to their Jewish heritage, no matter how much they identified as Hungarian and no matter how much they contributed to society, their place within it was never a given.

The first two generations of the Hungarian Holtzer family showed great ingenuity in the face of discrimination and did well to even start a business, to build a life for their families. Trading on the streets and from their homes were acts of survival. It is no surprise that Jakob, the third-generation immigrant, placed so much value on the business and on owning property. Knowing that his father lived in a time when none of this was possible, he wouldn't have taken any of it for granted. Jakob and Julia worked tirelessly amid a constant deluge of legal and social discrimination to build S. Holtzer & Sons into the impressive empire that it was, for a brief moment in history.

This brief moment coincides with what historians refer to as the 'Golden Era', a window spanning roughly fifty years in which the Hungarian ruling classes – the upper classes and conservative aristocratic leadership – adopted a tolerant position towards the Jews, because it suited them for economic and political reasons at the time.

Stephen was born into these ebbing and flowing waves of anti-semitism, where unrest was the norm. Wealth safely passed down from one generation to the next is not the Jewish story and it is not the tale my family tree tells. Theirs is a story of immigration, of assimilation, of ascension despite constant discrimination, and of quick, brutal descent. Ultimately, the privileges Jakob and Julia worked so hard to obtain were fleeting and no amount of real estate, shop branches, charity work or coats of arms could save the family from what was to come.

CHAPTER 7

For the Time Being

I put my neck in the noose and went back to Hungary.
It's a long train journey from the west coast of Italy to Budapest. Along the way, Stephen goes over all the excuses he gave Katica as to why going to America would have been a bad idea.

'I don't know anyone there' was a flat-out lie. Of course, he knows several musicians and people in the film industry who moved to America to achieve greater or escape lesser fortunes. He goes through them in his mind, picturing a life among them and thinking which of the tenuous connections and acquaintances might have grown into friendships in this alternate reality.

'I don't have any of my belongings with me!' Without papers, Stephen thinks it unlikely that he would be granted permission to stay in America. He is not a refugee, he has told his mother. He also thinks it impractical to emigrate without taking with him any of his possessions.

'How am I going to survive over there? I don't have that much money' was a far cry from his earlier exuberant self, raising his hands in front of his parents, assured in himself and his abilities.

'I have a contract to fulfil!' This was true. Stephen is under contract to accompany Alvia Suli at The Dunacorzo for the fast approaching summer season.

'I have shows to play' and 'I can't leave my family' are the thoughts he holds on to, repeating them in his mind like a mantra, until the train pulls in to Budapest.

In music, repetition is important. Repeating a certain melody or hook throughout a song helps unify the melody and makes any given piece of music more accessible to the listener. It's the melodic equivalent to a steady beat. Similarly, we need repetition, or routine, in our lives. If the shows at the restaurant are the recurring motif, Stephen's family and Katica in particular are the root note, pulling Stephen back home and back to normality.

For a while, Stephen slips comfortably into a routine of composing and rehearsing. Throughout, he is preoccupied with thoughts of Roszi. Although he doesn't say it, I'm certain that the hope of potentially reconciling with her was another pull that beckoned him back home to Budapest. Almost every day, Stephen swings by the Grand Hotel Royal, the current hot spot and main hang-out for Budapest's film and theatre folk, on the off-chance that he might find Roszi there.

By then, I was really sick that I have let her go.

Stephen has wished for the scene to unfold before his eyes for so long that when it does, it takes a full moment for him to fully realise it. As he walks into the courtyard of the hotel, he sees Roszi sitting at one of the round, metal tables with another woman. In this moment, all defences drop. He rushes towards her and falls to his knees. Unabashed and unperturbed by the stranger sitting at the table or the many socialites watching on, Stephen begs for Roszi's forgiveness and for her to come back to him.

Roszi, like Stephen, had undoubtedly played this scene over in her mind, thinking it likely that they would meet again, given the smallness of their social circles. But she wasn't prepared for this uncharacteristic display of vulnerability. She exchanges quick, furtive glances with her friend, while Stephen pleads with her.

'Istvan, please,' she says in a bid to calm him. With a sad smile, she goes on to explain kindly and patiently that she can't possibly return to him, that Stephen surely understands. As his pleading continues, her tone grows sterner.

'It is not possible any more,' she says, staring at him intently. 'It is for the best.'

He falls quiet and nods at her, before stepping away. Stephen feels the wound in his chest expand as he retreats to take a seat at a table facing away from her.

Once he accepts that he will not be able to win her back, Stephen decides to move out of his bachelor pad, where they had lived and been happy together. In pursuit of a fresh start, he moves back across the river from Buda to Pest, renting a studio flat in the fashionable, newly built Leopold Town. While most of Budapest's architecture consists of ornate, Baroque-style tenement houses, Leopold Town was built in the modern, German-inspired Bauhaus style of design. With an easy commute to the town centre, Leopold Town attracts mostly working professionals, the vast majority of whom happened to be Jewish.

Stephen and Roszi will run into one another several times after this encounter. The former lovers will exchange niceties and remain in amicable, albeit superficial, contact before eventually drifting apart. It is Katica who stays in touch with Roszi. In the near future, Stephen will learn from his mother that Roszi has fallen in love with a cameraman and that they will go on to marry and have a baby boy.

* * *

I stayed and played until I got the call-up: railway building in Transylvania.

One morning after a particularly late night, three months after choosing home over America, Stephen notices a menacingly official-looking envelope that must have been carelessly shoved through the letterbox the previous day. Bleary-eyed, he bends down slowly to pick it up. Inspecting it suspiciously, his eyes stay focused on the letter as he moves through the flat and slumps down on a green embroidered armchair that has his black dinner jacket draped over the back of it from the night before.

Stephen is being summoned to what the letter refers to as 'military training'. It states that he is one of a handful of Hungarians who missed conscription in younger years – in Stephen's case, most likely, because he was abroad at the time. He is instructed to report to a railway station in Fot, a small village in the Pest County north of Budapest Central, in three weeks' time. The 'military training' is to take place in Hungary's newly annexed North Transylvania and will take three months, from mid-September through to mid-December.

There is something about the letter that strikes Stephen as odd, but in the moment, he cannot tell whether it is the contents or his hangover that is to blame. Cross-referencing with some of his acquaintances, who received similar notifications, he accepts it. After all, with surrounding countries already at war, Stephen doesn't think it unlikely that Hungary will want to prepare its citizens to fight. It isn't too long ago that Lorant was conscripted – he remembers his brother's reports of his military training. That too had lasted three months. During that time, Lorant learned to handle a rifle, how to fashion a mattress out of straw, and how to march in formation. With his brother's experience in mind and a conscious memory of his father serving for his country, it will not have been too far outside of Stephen's reality.

In Hungary, the labour-service system was introduced twenty years prior to Stephen's call-up. Initially, it was designed for any men of so-called military age who were deemed unfit to bear arms for one reason or another and wasn't necessarily discriminatory in nature. Up until this point in time, labour-service men were paid the same as those in the military, were clothed, fed and generally taken care of. Perhaps it was knowledge of this, or a dose of bravado, that leads Stephen to show little concern. He goes ahead with preparations for this unexpected interruption to the autumn season. Stephen gets to packing and informs his friends, employers and colleagues that, from September through to December, he will be otherwise engaged and will not be able to perform. He reluctantly informs Alvia and The Dunacorzo that he will not be able to join them for the autumn season and arranges to rejoin them for the winter season at the beginning of December.

Unbeknownst to Stephen, his call-up coincides with a pivotal moment: the Hungarian government take a sharp turn to the right, bowing to both internal and external political pressures in the realisation that the Third Reich wants something in return for the land it gave back to Hungary.

Precisely when Stephen is called up for what he somewhat jokingly refers to as 'so-called forced labour' in his retelling, the existing laws around labour services are used by Hungarian's now far-right government as a legal basis to make such work compulsory, manipulating them to target a specific group of people. The actual forced labour was almost secondary to the main goal: to remove Jews from cultural and socioeconomic life.

When Stephen arrives at the station in Fot, he recognises a few of the faces assembled with him – acquaintances from all disparate corners of his life, such as the tennis club, fellow musicians and family friends. Among the men, Stephen spots one of his friends, the slightly taller and considerably more studious Laslo Somogyi. Laslo's family also works in textiles, but unlike Stephen, Laslo has found his vocation in the business and has worked hard to set up his own textile shop, which he runs with his wife. As the two men spy one another, they embrace and chat before boarding the train. Overall, the atmosphere on the station platform is more akin to excitement ahead of an excursion, a small adventure providing a momentary distraction from busy lives. As they board the train, Stephen notices a camera dangling from a thick leather strap across Laslo's neck.

'Going to take some nice holiday pictures?' Stephen laughs.

'Something like that . . . I thought I'd document our adventure,' Laslo says, tucking the camera inside his jacket.

Laslo tells Stephen that, through connections, he's managed to get a position as personal assistant to their commanding officer. He will be performing various administrative and secretarial tasks instead of physical labour. As such, he thought he might have the opportunity to document his experience.

The train journey takes most of the day. In a moment where he and Laslo exhaust small talk, Stephen closes his eyes. Even if the next months are stealing precious time away from performing and composing, Stephen thinks, at least he'll be in good company.

Upon arrival, it strikes the men as odd that they are not given uniforms or equipped with tools. Instead, they are forced to wear armbands bearing the Star of David, marking them as Jews – most wear yellow, those who are converted Christians wear white.

I don't really know why that distinction was given, Stephen says, *we all had to do the same physical work.*

Perhaps predictably, no one in Stephen's group has any prior experience in laying railway tracks. The work is hard, manual labour, involving the emptying of swamps and laying of heavy, iron railway lines, and only a few of the men in the group are physically up for the job. Their clothes, waistcoats and spectacles are more appropriate for an evening out in the town as opposed to working ten-hour shifts, carrying and hammering railway lines.

Well, it looked like a humorous affair.

It comes as a relief that, while the work is hard, there is no violent disciplining or even close supervision. While the men dutifully fulfil their daily tasks, heaving metal across the emptied swamp in mud-stained leather shoes, their commanding officer spends most of his time busying himself with paperwork in his village house. Laslo is quick to pick up on the fact that the officer deems being in charge of a civilian group such as they are, to be beneath him. While to me it seems infinitely more desirable to perform administrative duties, Stephen doesn't envy Laslo's position. Among various other tasks, his duties include emptying the commanding officer's chamber pot.

I would not have fancied myself to carry and empty the captain's night pot. I preferred rather to work, but this wish soon proved to be harder than I expected.

Although the work is hard, it is 'nothing like it was later', the older Stephen in the tapes confesses.

A few of us made friends – Laslo Somogyi among us – I think we were seven who became close.

Stephen, in his own words, is 'strong as an ox', all those years training in boxing, swimming and tennis coming in handy. Only on one occasion does he come close to meeting his physical limits: one piece of iron railway is so heavy, he has to call for more men to come and help him. It takes eight of them to lift it. There's an autumnal chill in the air, but Stephen and his colleagues have discarded their overcoats, now shirtless and sweating, suspenders dangling around their strained calves as they group together to try to carry it to its destination. With a thud, it falls to the ground and, after a second of mopping brows and uttering an assortment of choice swear words, they all kneel down to hammer it into place. A yell from the commanding officer signals their long-awaited lunch break. Trudging through mud, the men climb out of the cleared swamp and towards the soup kitchen, set up in what looks like old ruins along the hillside. Ahead, Laslo Somogyi has his camera raised in front of his face. As he snaps the men queuing to collect their daily bread, one of the men calls out to him.

'Laslo! Is your wife coming to see you?'

Laslo turns around, cradling the camera: 'Yes! Edith . . . What about yours?'

As an unmarried man, no one had thought it necessary to inform Stephen that spouse visitation was permitted. Homesick, he has an idea.

'Hey . . . hey, Laslo!' Stephen steals his friend's attention from the group.

'Can Edith not bring Katica? My mother? She could pick her up and they could travel together from Budapest?'

'I don't see why not.' Laslo shrugs and joins the end of the queue. 'I'll see if I can reach her and I'll ask.'

Lost in thought, Stephen starts to follow Laslo. With all the gigging and travelling, he has hardly spent time with his family since he first left for Switzerland two years ago and the prospect of seeing his mother is enough to get him through the following weeks.

Can you imagine what liberties we had! Six wives to seven friends were allowed to visit!

At the end of October, halfway through the deployment, Stephen and the other labourers are permitted leave for the occasion. For a day, they are free to receive visitors, to explore the nearby village and to get a proper meal from the local amenities if they so choose. This makes for a welcome change to the usual bowl of soup from an outdoor kitchen. The hard, manual labour, Stephen can accept and take in his stride – but as someone who cherishes the finer things in life, the slop served up as a daily meal he finds intolerable.

The small village in Transylvania's Kolozs County is quiet. It is a cold but sunny day as Stephen and Laslo head over to the rustic hotel restaurant where they've arranged to meet Edith and Katica. They wait for quite some time in good spirits, perusing the menu, debating what they should order and discussing the likelihood of the wine being any good. A bushy beard now covers Stephen's normally clean-shaven face. He's rather fond of it and, to his surprise, it's growing out with a tinge of orange. For a moment he muses to himself whether Katica will even recognise him. In his imagined scenario, he has to wave at her from across the restaurant before she smiles, after doing a double-take at her son's rugged appearance.

With a creak, the door opens and Edith walks in. She looks a little weary from the journey, her slim, angular face flushed from the cold and her gloved hands clutching her long coat closed at her chest. As Laslo jumps up and hurries towards the entrance to greet his wife, the realisation sets in that Katica is not with her.

THE PIANO PLAYER OF BUDAPEST

'Istvan, this is Edith.' Laslo, knowing his friend, recognises Stephen's stony facial expression, predicting the inevitable outburst that is sure to follow.

Stephen manages a barely detectable nod and remains silent, slumped in his seat, all previous joviality now drained from him.

I am familiar with those split seconds in which I attempt to process emotions, a toing and froing of thought so fast, it's almost imperceptible to even myself. After a moment of silent, internal debate, during which Edith and Laslo contemplate the menu on the opposite side of the table, Stephen decides against keeping his composure: 'Where's my mother? Why didn't you bring her?'

'I think it would have been too strenuous a journey for her, don't you?' While Edith's tone is stern, she stays calm, contrary to her opponent. This only leads Stephen to raise his voice even further.

'I think that this wasn't for you to decide,' he snaps and proceeds to sulk in solitude for the duration of the meal.

And so it happens that the first time my grandparents meet, they have a heated argument – one of many. Apparently, they never stopped arguing.

That is how we met and that is how we spoke.

That night, they all stay in the village bed and breakfast. After the restaurant, the couple bid hasty goodbyes to Stephen and retreat to their room.

I did not presume for a minute they wanted to play cards.

Stephen orders half a bottle of cognac at the bar and is suddenly intensely aware of his loneliness. Frustrated, he swipes the drink up from the counter and climbs up to his room. He lies down on the bed, but just as his head hits the thin pillow, there's a soft knock on the door. Stephen gets up and opens the door ever so slightly, to see

72

the maid. She sheepishly asks if there's anything she can do for him and he invites her in.

Laslo's good relations with the commanding officer prove beneficial to Stephen. By mid-November, he is growing increasingly worried about his contract at The Dunacorzo. The winter season is approaching and Stephen realises that he won't be back in time for the first shows in December. He tries his very best to explain himself to the commanding officer and Laslo puts in a good word for him. To the surprise of everyone, Stephen is granted leave for a few days to fulfil his contract in Budapest, on condition that he returns within the week to complete the remaining fortnight of labour in Transylvania.

Once back in Budapest, I just did not return to call-up.

Stephen does not hear from the authorities and assumes he's got away with cutting his forced labour short without further consequences. He happily forgets about the railway tracks and the daily slop and continues with his life. He swiftly loses touch with the new friends he made in Transylvania – *We did not see each other until much later*, Stephen informs us. In his words, *everything went back to normal . . .* There's a long pause in which I can hear the click of the tape as he hits the pause and record button to add, *for the time being.*

CHAPTER 8

They Danced until Doomsday

There are an infinite number of melodies within a finite number of notes. When I was a child, I would play the piano unaware that my fingers were pressing the same keys as Stephen's had so many years before me. But I was in awe of the sound reverberating from them, knowing, but not understanding, that a new combination of notes could always be found and that an unsung melody could always be unearthed. Paternal fingers placing infant ones on middle C, the third above and the fifth note above that, my dad guided me through the basics of music theory. It would largely remain a foreign language to me, much as Hungarian had been to my dad. He was much more successful in teaching me how to be free, to find happiness in singing, playing, learning and collaborating. It is a strange comfort to me that Stephen was the same. In his music, he too was free, confident in his ability to feel, to improvise and create music without the confinements of theory or too serious a schooling. I imagine that he too grew addicted to the rush of finding a new melody, creating something out of nothing that resonates with others.

Throughout 1941, Stephen commits himself to songwriting, building an impressive portfolio of compositions for a future in music that was never meant to be. This is the most fruitful time in his life as a composer, the crescendo of his creative output mirroring that of the rising political tension and impending catastrophe.

He works with a number of lyricists, who put words to Stephen's music. The most significant collaboration is with Ivan Szenes. There is something special about the collaboration between Stephen and Ivan, who is only sixteen years old. Despite his young age, lyricism comes naturally to him. He inherited this gift from his father Andor, who has just passed away prematurely. Andor was a good friend of Aladar's, and Stephen has fond memories of playing music together with him at family parties when the Holtzer Bastyais first moved to Budapest. It was Andor's wife who suggested the pair should collaborate in memory and honour of Andor. Stephen loves the idea and agrees immediately. At their first writing session, Stephen tells Ivan of the time he and his father had, albeit somewhat jokingly, started writing a musical comedy together. 'Wouldn't it be special if we made it a reality?'

The pair get to work, writing in Stephen's studio apartment as well as at the Blüthner piano in St Stephen's Square. At the latter location, they enjoy hearty dinners with Katica and Aladar, who are always keen to hear the melodies composed that day. They write a number of songs together and, whenever they get stuck or need a break, chip away at outlining the musical comedy. Together, they land a publishing deal for several of their songs, which are recorded by various singers, as well as orchestras.

I have some tapes of them so anyone who's interested can hear them!

'I'm interested!' I shout out loud and pause the tape. It feels so intimate listening to Stephen, getting to spend time with him, that, for a brief moment, I forget that my grandfather can't actually hear me. I thumb through the cassette tapes I have with me in London, but I can't find these compositions. I make a mental note to ask my sister and Aunt Julie if they might know where they are or if they even exist.

In spring 1941, Stephen's contract at The Dunacorzo accompanying Alvia Suli comes to an end. Like Irene and Istvan, she too has decided to move, to seek out the safety of America. On one of their last nights performing together, she requests Stephen play the popular Hungarian song 'Gloomy Sunday'. Although it was written in 1936, it would soon become a world-wide hit thanks to Billie Holiday's more jazzy rendition. That's the thing about songs – you never know when they might resonate and ride an unexpected wave towards global success. The song is dark, so much so that it is often referred to as Hungary's suicide song. Urban myth has it that hundreds of Hungarians have taken their own lives while listening to it. Over the next couple of years, the song will become so renowned throughout the western world for its darkness, that the BBC will ban it from its airwaves, deeming it bad for wartime morale. Alvia, being the character singer she is, adds a comical, almost absurd twist to it. With an exaggerated hand gesture, she points to her left towards the Danube, inferring jumping in and drowning to match the lyric:

Angels have no thought
Of ever returning you,
Would they be angry
If I thought of joining you?

On 3 April 1941, Hungarian Prime Minister Count Pal Teleki commits suicide. Stephen reads it in the newspaper. At first, everyone is puzzled as to why he would take his own life.

'I remember him being a very nice person and very knowledgeable,' writes Lorant in a telegram to his parents. Lorant used to be a student of Teleki's back when Teleki was a professor of geography at Budapest's university, and he is sad to hear of his passing. The news shakes the country and rumours soon start to spin whether there might have been foul play at hand. The details will take a while to emerge.

What actually happened was that the Hungarian Prime Minister had recently signed a peace agreement with Yugoslavia and found himself in a bind when Germany put pressure on him to allow German troops to pass through Hungary in order to invade. Meanwhile, Britain was threatening diplomatic sanctions should he not stand up to the Germans. Faced with two bad choices, Teleki made a third and ended his own life. His suicide note reads: 'We broke our word out of cowardice . . . The nation feels it, and we have thrown away its honour. We have allied ourselves to scoundrels . . . We will become body-snatchers! A nation of trash. I did not hold you back. I am guilty.'

Lorant's fondness of Teleki embodies the complexity of personal and the fickleness of political identity. It is important to note that Teleki was acting out of blind nationalism, rather than any kind of moral superiority. Earlier in his political career, during times of peace and prosperity for Hungary, Teleki's attitude towards Jews was one of acceptance, at least towards those who had fully assimilated. At the time, he stated that 'from a social point of view, the Hungarian Jews are not Jews any more but Hungarians'. It was fair-weather support, for his attitude changed as soon as political unrest was on the rise and Hungary's borders were under threat. Suddenly, he saw Jews as a 'problem of life and death for the Hungarian people'. In fact, it was he who passed the first antisemitic laws after the First World War, restricting the number of Jewish students allowed to attend university. Ironically, Lorant, one of his favourite students, was one of them.

Shortly after Teleki's death, Lorant is called back to join the army. It is his job to drive the lorry leading the convoy into Yugoslavia. When they arrive after an eight-hour drive, Yugoslavian villagers greet them with the Hungarian national colours and throw blue lilacs into the windows of the vehicles.

While the death of Teleki is big news, *on the whole*, Stephen remarks, *there seemed to be no change in Hungary.*

That is not to say that there aren't growing tensions and concerns among the public. Germany and its allies begin invading the Soviet Union. To what extent Hungary should participate is a hot topic in Hungarian politics. At the end of June, the new Prime Minister, László Bárdossy, with support from Regent Horthy (who has been serving as the regent of the Kingdom of Hungary since 1920), declares war on the Soviet Union.

Stephen notes a significant influx of Jewish refugees from Germany, Austria and Poland arriving in Budapest. As alarming as the slow-travelling news of Hitler's atrocities against Jews is, the fact that so many of those able to flee are seeking refuge here further validates Stephen's belief that he and his family are safe within his beloved Hungary.

This belief is challenged for the first time when, with summer coming to a close, Stephen returns to the mountains. He takes a contract in the north Hungarian mountain region of Kekes in a hotel mostly occupied by army officers and generals – a distinctly different clientele to the left-leaning art, theatre and music lovers who usually enjoy Stephen's music. He pulls up to the hotel, disembarks from the coach and walks up the driveway. The uniformed staff greet him, arms raised, in a Nazi salute. He freezes. It is hard, in this moment, for Stephen to hide the shock on his face.

There is a danger in homogeny. The company Stephen tends to keep, the Bohemians and intellectuals, and the circles he moves within have instilled in him a false sense of security. Up until this point, his melodies played within a beautiful, but dangerous echo chamber. His own countrymen greeting Stephen with a German 'Heil Hitler' salute comes as a terrible surprise. He recovers from the shock, but cannot sleep that night. He lies awake in his room, thinking of all the things he would prefer to have said or done in response to the salute and is annoyed at himself for having frozen. Stephen fulfils his contract, which lasts somewhere between six to eight weeks. Unlike at his other engagements, he limits socialising to a minimum and largely remains alone in between sets, not wanting to attract attention. He has no desire for political debate or confrontation and so he keeps his head down, staring at the black and white of the piano keys as he plays, instead of engaging with the room.

I was not sorry to leave – it was an eye-opener.

As much as Stephen is holding on to the threads of his pre-war life, the rise in tension is undeniable. On 6 December, he travels further up the mountain and arrives at Hotel Kekes. The highest resort in altitude and prestige alike is nestled in the snow-covered, treeless peaks. Here, the predominantly Jewish clientele spend the winter months skiing and enjoying the amenities the resort has to offer, the very best of live music being one of them. Stephen is thrilled to have landed the contract. Hotel Kekes is renowned for treating its artists well. Stephen slips and slides towards the entrance on the icy ground, the staff welcome him and show him around the establishment. As he settles in his room to unpack and get ready for his evening performance, he hears on the radio that Britain has declared war on Hungary.

A great performer has to be highly attuned to emotions in order to read and entertain a room. As Stephen begins performing at Hotel Kekes, he is quick to pick up on a frenetic energy. What follows is an evening of delicate push and pull – he plays a soft minor key as he notices people huddled in hushed conversation. He looks out into the room and sees worried faces, some, he can make out, are holding back tears. While he plays, he watches audience members reading and sharing copies of the newspaper, pointing at certain lines and exchanging anxious glances. As the evening progresses, the mood changes. It is an atmosphere of cognitive dissonance and heightened emotion. As the clientele order bottle after bottle, Stephen picks up in tempo, leading his audience to the dance floor and into the night.

In those first weeks of December, the world seems to spin faster, each day bringing with it an extraordinary amount of upheaval on a global scale. Japan bombs Pearl Harbor. America declares war on Japan, on Germany and its allies. Germany, in turn, declares war on America. Russia retaliates against Germany's attacks on Moscow. Hitler declared the 'Night and Fog' decree, which is directed against anyone in occupied territories who in any way undermines German war efforts. Those who do not comply are now punishable by death. Hitler misappropriated the name for the decree – it comes from Germany's most famous poet, Wolfgang Goethe, who used the phrase to mean clandestine actions concealed by fog and the darkness of the night.

And throughout this turmoil, Stephen plays piano – sometimes a song of defiance, sometimes a lamenting melody, while the Hungarian Jewish gentry dance, drink and sing. Despite the speed at which the world is turning, Stephen has a great time performing at Hotel Kekes. Perhaps he feels in his bones that it will be a while before he is able to perform again. And so, Stephen soaks up every minute of playing and after-hour indulgences. At the top of the mountain, he often plays throughout the night, watching the sunrise and the tip jar overflow. The lively and appreciative audience spoils Stephen, throwing their money at the musician, for fear of what tomorrow might bring.

I had cases of cognac and whisky sent to me and I needed it! To keep up with the non-stop playing, I consumed a minimum of one bottle a night.

It was fascinating to watch and to be part of the self-delusion, he reflects, *but at the same time, the fear of what the future is holding for us all, assembled at Hotel Kekes.*

Throughout the winter season, many of his friends and family members take weekend trips up the mountain to see him play and to keep him company. Among the many visitors are Laslo and Edith Somogyi.

Stephen is already several glasses of wine into the evening when he spots Laslo in the audience. In his break from playing, he walks up to him, arms outstretched. Laslo demonstratively pushes himself up from his chair and steps forward to greet Stephen.

'What are you doing here?' Stephen asks, his tone conveying pleasant surprise.

'Well, we had a night off and have heard good things about the live music here,' Laslo replies.

Stephen is genuinely touched by the surprise and is all the more embarrassed at the social faux pas that follows: when he tipsily turns to Edith, he mistakes her for his cousin's wife Tecla. A shy Edith simply smiles in reply when he greets her with a wrong name, before he realises his error and apologises profusely. After the awkward moment passes, he joins them for a drink and small talk, before it is time for him to get back to work. He quickly orders a bottle of wine to be sent to the Somogyi table before he slides back onto the comfort of his piano stool and breaks into a sultry instrumental version of Duke Ellington's 'I Got It Bad (And That Ain't Good)'.

As the days pass, the nights at Hotel Kekes become ever more raucous. He remembers the resolve in the eyes of audience members, as they dance a knowing last dance, drawing the nights out for as long as they could. Reflecting on the scenes, Stephen references the Old Testament and compares the Jewish gentry's escapism to the newly freed Egyptian slaves. It's the part in the Old Testament where Moses heads up the mountain to receive a message from God. The more time passes, the more people start to lose faith and doubt whether he will return. Distraught, they give in to hedonism and debauchery – basically having a massive party – until their saviour returns to lead them out of the desert. It is far from a perfect analogy, but it implies that everyone was aware of the dark on the horizon and that, at Hotel Kekes, they drank, sang and danced in the face of it.

There was NO MOSES NOW, Stephen writes, *so they danced until doomsday came.*

Stephen's contract ends with the thawing of the ice. He leaves Hotel Kekes on 10 April 1942 and returns to Budapest just in time to wave off his brother Lorant, who has once again been called up to head east with the Hungarian Army. This time, their destination is Ukraine, transporting supplies to support the Hungarian war efforts on the Soviet front. There is a photograph in Stephen's album of Lorant's convoy, a long snake of lorries and cars driving out of

Budapest. In the margins, it reads: 'Lorant convoy into Russia: 1942.' The photo appears to be taken from a vantage point, as though Stephen and his family had gathered to wave Lorant good-bye and to wish him well.

In the spring of 1942, Hungary goes through yet another major political change. Prime Minister Bárdossy is replaced by the more moderate Kallay. It is an attempt by the Hungarian government to create some distance between itself and Hitler's regime. Elsewhere in Europe, Jews are already forced to wear the 'yellow star' in public and, unbeknownst to Stephen, Germany is increasing the pressure on Hungary's government, demanding they enforce the same harsh regulations and hand over their Jewish citizens to them. For now, there is resistance and Stephen is free to continue life.

I made so much more in tips than my actual fee, Stephen reflects. *When I came down from the mountain, I had so much money, I didn't know what to do with it.*

With his excess income, he splurges on fashion, buying himself and his parents the finest coats, shoes, hats and shirts available. He buys and swiftly consumes bottles of high-end wines and cognacs. Stephen tries to continue performing, spending the majority of the summer in a tireless loop of playing solo in smaller clubs, bars and restaurants around Pest. These gigs are far less formal and sporadic. Venues are no longer offering contracts – with the war so close, long-term commitments are rendered useless. Life suddenly feels a cruel limbo, the pervasive sense among most that seismic pressures could reach boiling point any day now.

THEN IT HAPPENED, Stephen writes in capitals. *I was called up. This time we all felt, and knew, this is the real thing.*

In October 1942, Stephen is one of 1,070 Jewish Hungarian men to be called up to provide forced labour on the Russian war front.

The letter instructs Stephen to report to a train station in a northern part of Hungary. He is permitted to take one rucksack and is advised to bring warm clothes.

A song unsung is that of parting. There is a noticeable absence of emotion in Stephen's retelling of this moment in time. He does not mention saying goodbye to his parents. I know it must have taken place – a mournful last evening together, the air heavy with sorrow and worry. There must have been a final run of fingers along the keys of the Blüthner piano.

When the dreaded morning comes, Stephen swings his rucksack over his shoulders and closes the front door to his apartment block in Leopold Town. En route to Budapest's station, he runs into his Uncle Emil, who looks his nephew up and down and asks gruffly: 'Is that what you're wearing?'

'What do you mean?' Stephen pipes back naively.

'Istvan, you're going to Russia and you're wearing a three-quarter-length raincoat!' He points with exasperation at his nephew's attire.

'It was fine in Transylvania! I'll be all right, don't worry.' Stephen smiles reassuringly.

'Well.' Emil takes a moment to search for the right parting words: 'You show those Russians what we Hungarians are made of!'

Perhaps Emil, much like his nephew, is still dangerously underestimating the threat inching towards them. Or maybe his uncle's goodbye is meant as a rallying cry. Sometimes, belief to the point of denial is all we have to hold on to.

I met again the same people, with whom I was in Transylvania – all seven of us together again – this time there were no smiles.

Stephen assembles together with hundreds of men in North Hungary, near the Czechoslovakian border. As he looks around, he suddenly feels underdressed, noticing that everyone else is wrapped in thick winter coats and hefting bags that look much heavier than his.

At the assembly place, they are divided into five companies, 250 men in each. *If I remember well*, Stephen says and proceeds to list the group numbers: *109/38, 109/39, 109/40, 109/41, 109/42 – I think I was in group 109/40.* At this time the groupings seem merely administrative in purpose.

Little did we know, Stephen says, *that for most, this meant the death warrant.*

The following morning, after a night of rough sleep in a camp, Stephen and 1,069 other men, all of them Jewish artists and business owners, are shoved into cattle wagons. The voice of a soldier permeates the wagon as everyone's head turns towards the barked instructions: 'Do you see this man?' The soldier points at a seemingly random person standing closest to the door. 'If anyone tries to escape from the train, this man is going to be shot, okay? So remember that, if you're going to try to weasel your way out of your duty.'

Wide-eyed, panicked glances are exchanged, before the door to the wagon is slammed shut and the train jolts forward.

PART TWO

Survival

CHAPTER 9

You Weren't Warm Enough

They put us in cattle wagons and bolted the doors shut. Stephen's voice is slower and monotone. He instantly sounds older and more fragile.

Imagination and memory are wonderfully strange beasts. I had internalised this chapter of his story at such an early age that my memory of it remained childlike. I somehow always pictured that train journey to be a train journey as I know it – with seats and handrails, possibly even a beverage along the way. As I'm listening to this digitised tape recording, I happen to be on a train, heading up from London Marylebone to the West Midlands to visit my Aunt Julie, but with those two words – cattle wagons – that false image stored for so long shatters. Stephen's tone is laboured, as if for him, too, uttering those words somehow breaks something within him all over again.

Stephen doesn't know, as he stands in the crowded darkness of the cattle wagon, that he isn't expected to return. He and the other 1,069 are being sent as collateral, a sinister deal between the Hungarian and German governments.

Hungary may have protected its Jewish population up to this point, but it has ultimately caved, handing over Budapest's elite and sending them out to perish in Russia.

Sending them to the front for forced labour not only helps satisfy the requirements of the military, it also fulfils certain ideological objectives, including the so-called 'solution' of the Jewish question. It targets those who play a significant role in their communities; special attention is given to calling up the rich, the prominent professionals, the thinkers, the artists, as well as religious leaders. The change in policy is palpable to Stephen in the tension between the supervising soldiers and the forced labourers. It pierces the atmosphere like a cold, sharp blade.

As the cattle wagon pulls out of the station, its wheels screeching in the tracks, the dread that has been building up for months seems to clog Stephen's inners like a thick sediment. Judging by the nervous and despondent looks around him, others feel the same – shoulders against shoulders, heads dart around in the dark, in search of the random man who would pay with his life, should any of them attempt to escape.

Stephen's thoughts don't seem to have much time to settle. Before he is able to acclimatise to his strange surroundings, the train begins to slow. Surely, we must still be in Hungary, he thinks. They come to a screeching halt, stopping at the last station before the Slovakian border. At first he thinks he is imagining it, but then, the voice grows louder and clearer.

'Bastyai? Bastyai, Istvan?' The voice must belong to a man walking along the length of train, searching for him.

'Yes! Here,' Stephen responds, hesitant at first, craning his neck to face the bolted door, through which he can hear the disembodied voice as those around him turn to look at Stephen and one another with a hushed unease. With a jolt and a loud creak, the wagon door slides open, light flooding the carriage.

'Bastyai, Istvan?' the voice now bellows, projecting directly into the overcrowded wagon.

'Here!' Stephen shouts, imbuing his voice with as much confidence as he can muster.

'Step outside,' the voice commands, 'quickly!'

With great difficulty, Stephen pushes his way through the crowd of men and steps out on to the platform. The voice, he can now see, belongs to a portly, uniformed man.

'Papers,' he says, his voice containing no clues as to what this is about. Stephen rummages through his rucksack and shows his call-up letter and passport for inspection. The man doesn't take the papers into his own hands. A mere glimpse, confirming the name, seems to suffice. He nods and turns around, motioning Stephen to follow him as they walk briskly towards the station house.

'You've got to be really quick, okay? We can't delay the train and you have to be back on it. Or else I will have to pay for it. Understood?'

Before Stephen has time to gather his thoughts, he sees them. There, in the station house, are his parents. Katica and Aladar look anxious and tired, as though they haven't slept in days. The overriding emotion Stephen reads on their faces, though, is relief. This moment, in all its incredulity, seems to last both an eternity and a mere split second.

I don't know why I knew to hug my dad with such intention. We had so many really good, meaningful hugs. Some were on ordinary days, to say goodnight after a fun evening of making music together, staying up much later than I should have on a school night. Others were more poignant, saying goodbye at Berlin's airport departure drop-off car park when he was already ill and I had to leave, back to my compartmentalised life in England. For every single one of those hugs, I was present in that moment. I would soak up the embrace, determined to commit each aspect of it to my long-term memory, to store it in my being and to give and feel as much love as I could. The strange thing is that sometimes now, the sensations of that hug will come rushing over my body, seemingly out of nowhere. When I'm either desperately sad or exceptionally jubilant, I feel them. My body suddenly and magically fills with the overwhelming feeling of hugging my dad. There is nothing akin to a physical embrace by those we love the most.

In this moment, Stephen, Katica and Aladar embrace. They cry. They kiss. They cup faces in hands. Before Stephen can find any words to make sense of what is happening, his mother thrusts a thick, sheepskin coat into his hands.

'You were not warm enough,' she says.

With those parting words and a last, hurried embrace, Stephen is ushered back on to the train and Aladar and Katica watch him leave, standing perfectly still until they can't hear the wheels rattle along the northbound tracks any longer. They thank the commanding officer and get back into the taxi waiting for them outside the station to drive them back to Budapest.

The cattle wagon continues its journey, travelling north-east, stopping only occasionally for 'relieving oneself', as Stephen says, or for a quick food break, during which a mobile soup kitchen pulls up next to the train. It becomes harder for Stephen to keep a sense of time with little to no light breaching the wagon, in which there is barely enough space to sit on the floor when his legs grow tired. Soon, he loses track entirely, unsure of how many days they have been on the move.

Word travels fast in families. Unbeknownst to Stephen, his uncle stopped by Katica's and Aladar's home immediately after his shift to inform them that their son's idea of 'warm clothes' was a thin, three-quarter-length raincoat.

Katica, appalled at the news, jumps into action. As Stephen arrives at the camp in Northern Hungary, she hurries to pawn some of her jewellery. With the cash in hand, she runs to a tailor nearest to their office and commissions him to make the warmest coat he can and as fast as possible. Within twenty-four hours, the sheepskin coat, lined with thick, cream-coloured wool, is ready. With the remaining cash, Aladar and Katica pay for a taxi, bribing the driver to go faster than is safe, in order to chase and overtake the train their son is on.

Mothers do have a strange ability to intuit. I've seen mine jump into action at an otherworldly pace, as if pulled by a magical thread the rest of us can't see. I'm sure Katica will have been the same – her motherly superpowers guiding her at lightning speed. It really is an incredible stroke of luck or, as Stephen calls it, the first of many 'helping hands from God', that Katica and Aladar manage to arrive at the train station at the Slovakian border ahead of the cattle wagon. It is an even greater good fortune that the officer in charge at the station happens to be an old acquaintance of Aladar's, and that he's able to convince him to give orders to stop the train, to allow Stephen to step out, for just that moment.

It's true – no amount of money or social status would have saved Stephen from being sent out to Russia, but at least in this instance there was jewellery to be pawned and contacts to lean on, in order to rectify Stephen's foolishness. Wearing the sheepskin coat, he will at least meet the Russian winter with a hope of survival.

The cattle wagon reaches its final destination. Once more, the bolted doors crash open, this time to a cacophony of angry voices, ordering the men to disembark. As they slowly shuffle on to the platform, the crunching of booted feet on fresh snow seems eerily loud. They are close to Stary Oskol, a small Russian town roughly 600km south of Moscow. The landscape around the station is bare, with nothing obscuring the horizon save for the endless sheet of grey-white snow. As Stephen looks around, he sees that some have come substantially better prepared than he had. A couple of men thought to bring sledges on which they are now strapping their bags in order to pull the weight behind them. Suddenly conscious of his idle hands, Stephen buttons up his coat. Craning his neck around him, he concludes that he is in better physical shape than most. It's dusk, but despite the falling of night and wintry cold, they are ordered to continue their journey on foot. He may not have thought to bring a sledge, he thinks, but at least he has his strength.

Following orders, they walk in a slightly south-eastern direction. Not in a neat single or double file – as their group is so large – but in a quiet, chaotic assembly. There is a tension in the air that seems to intensify the cold. How long are they expected to march for? What is their destination and what will await them there? The Hungarian soldiers don't communicate anything further than the barked orders to march and to keep marching, occasionally brandishing rifles and twirling batons in gloved hands. Not long into the walk, the first men begin to struggle, their rucksacks hanging heavy from their shoulders, making each step ever more cumbersome.

'Do you need help?' Stephen stretches a hand towards a man clearly his senior, gesturing to his rucksack.

'Istanem Igen' (God yes), the man replies, swiftly handing over his belongings with a nod of thanks and relief.

This gesture of kindness spreads. The men collaborate, taking it in turns to carry one another's bags to provide momentary relief for those who need it. They walk for hours. Now deep into the night, Stephen finds himself pulling two sledges, each with four to five bags upon it. He doesn't want to admit it, even to himself, but he is getting tired. He feels the night grow denser, the air colder, as his breathing becomes more laboured and his steps slower. There's still no end, no destination in sight. Just as he feels his exhaustion turn into anger, his brooding thoughts are interrupted.

There, seemingly out of nowhere, is a friendly, familiar face. Laslo Somogyi, sat on top of a horse.

'Hi!' He grins.

The Hungarian language is rich in swear words and Stephen utters a string of particularly colourful ones in shock at the unlikely scene before him.

'How?' he shouts, his arms outstretched in a violent shrug, momentarily forgetting the ache in his shoulders, before changing his mind. 'Do you know what? It's fine, I don't need to know.'

The horse, Stephen sees, is pulling a cart. Somehow, Laslo must have either happened upon and stolen a horse-drawn cart or managed to bribe someone – perhaps a nearby farmer – communicating via hand gestures. Either way, the relief Stephen feels as he and Laslo start heaving his sledges and rucksacks on to the horse-drawn cart is akin to hours of sleep. Once the cart is fully loaded, they utter a small, incredulous laugh and embrace before continuing into the night.

There's a commotion somewhere at the front of the group and a murmur filtering through to Laslo and Stephen. Someone has died. They don't know who, but soon they see him: a man, relatively small in stature, lies on the ground, face down. It was his heart, they're told by hushed voices.

'Do you know who he is?' Stephen asks Laslo, his eyes fixed on the lifeless body in the snow.

'No.' His voice is subdued.

'So what . . . do we just keep going?' Stephen asks incredulously as he and his friend watch others pass them by, their eyes firmly on the ground before them.

His question is soon answered by another sharp command of a soldier: 'Move it! Come on! Or do you want to join him?'

With a last glance at one another, they continue walking, leaving the unnamed stranger behind.

In the small hours of the morning, they eventually arrive at some form of shelter and are allowed to rest, but Stephen can't recall any details around what kind of place it was, nor can he say with any certainty exactly how far they were made to walk that first night. His memory is that of the shift among them once the death had occurred.

It was an amazing discovery, Stephen writes, *how the people can change from the time we have been put in the cattle wagons. The good-humoured, cultured, knowledgeable people changed into ruthless, heartless individuals, who stepped out of their old civilisation and gave all their energy, physical and mental, to self-preservation. So the death of this man was just taken by the others as something unimportant. Nobody could blame them*, he continues. *Only these circumstances, in which they were forced by other people.*

The following morning, Laslo's horse and cart are gone, along with the camaraderie among the men. From now on, everybody carries their own belongings. The walk continues throughout the day. They eventually arrive at their destination somewhere close to the River Don. They are put up in what Stephen refers to as 'peasant houses'. I imagine this to mean modest houses that either were abandoned or, perhaps more likely, had seen their owners forcibly removed by the Hungarian army. Stephen curls up on a free corner of the floor. He has a strong desire to wash and to change into fresh clothing, but there's no running water or heating and he is far too exhausted. As he tries to find a position comfortable enough to sleep, he notices for the first time an object in the inside pocket of his coat. Careful not to attract attention, he slowly looks down and slides a hand across the fabric. Inside lies a gold chain with an emerald four-leaf clover. Stephen, for a brief moment, feels a warmth – a motherly embrace. He tucks the chain safely back into his pocket and closes his eyes.

His sleep is soon rudely interrupted. It's dawn and angry voices permeate the house. They are ordering the men to assemble outside in the groups they had been assigned back in Hungary. I don't know how Stephen and Laslo parted ways that morning. I imagine they said goodbye in haste, perhaps a mere nod, the kind you give your friend when you expect to see them again in a short while. They weren't to know that the numbers they had been assigned became, in this moment, as Stephen later calls them, 'a deadly lottery'. However they parted, it would be the last interaction between them.

Each of the five divisions, made up of 214 men, was assigned a different task. For one of the groups, that allocation was an instant death sentence: they would be sent out to clear minefields. Two hundred and fourteen innocent Jewish lives were deemed a fair price for a clear field by the Hungarian army. While these men found a quick death, *the others*, Stephen writes years later, *had to wait for their time to come.*

CHAPTER 10

Chased and Hunted

Stephen grabs a heavy sack from the train that's just pulled in and, with a grunt, swings it over his shoulder. He struggles through the mud-soaked snow towards the pile of supply bags building up on the opposite end of the camp. With a dull thud, he lets it drop to the ground and runs back, as is demanded of him by the supervisors, and is quick to grab another sack to repeat the process.

Somewhere between Stary Oskol and the River Don, the group of 109/40 are in a forced labour camp working around the clock, loading and unloading munitions, provisions and other army supplies. There's no schedule: close to the frontline, trains arrive as and when. The work is brutal and relentless.

Stephen notices a younger man in his group working alongside him. He observes that he's carrying two, sometimes three, sacks at a time. Careful not to slow down, Stephen leans over and whispers to him as they draw level: 'Hey, why are you doing that? Carrying so many?'

The man looks alarmed, fearing what would happen if he is caught chatting. He whispers back through gritted teeth, avoiding looking Stephen directly in the eyes: 'I need them to know that I'm useful, you see? That I can work.'

Stephen understands and, as he reaches the train, immediately grabs two sacks. For hours he is forced to run back and forth, carrying these 50-100kg bags of cargo. All the while, the Hungarian soldiers jeer and hurl verbal abuse. Stephen soon understands why the man was so terrified to be spoken to. The soldiers walk along the length of the camp at a leisurely pace, carrying long, spiked sticks. Anyone who dares stop or slow down receives a heavy blow on their back.

For a moment, he foolishly believes that the setting of the sun might mean his shift is finally coming to an end, but as the daylight fades, the area is flooded with harsh, artificial spotlights and the work continues. In the night, temperatures plummet to minus degrees in the double digits. Civilian clothes do little to keep them warm in these conditions.

There is no shelter in the camp, save for one hut in which as many men as will fit huddle together to warm one another, while waiting for the next train of cargo to arrive. Their only source of heat is a wood-burning stove. With insufficient outlet for the smoke, keeping warm becomes a cruel game of endurance. You stay inside the hut for as long as you can stand the smoke. The spare scraps used to stoke the fire turn it into a thick, menacing cloud of black.

I can still smell that unbearable smoke, but it was a question to freeze or not.

After a gruelling eleven hours, soldiers order them to line up to receive their rations: a piece of bread and a bowl of watered-down soup, which turns from tepid to ice cold before the spoons reach mouths. They are marched to a village house near by. Its original inhabitants, Stephen guesses, will have fled or been forcibly removed. Everyone's quick to find a space on the floor, putting down small, rough blankets. Stephen sits, claiming the space beneath him. He covers himself with his sheepskin coat and closes his eyes. This gruelling routine fills Stephen's days and becomes his new reality.

I don't have a photograph of the camp, but somehow I have a clear image of it in my mind. A clearing, trees in a semicircle cupping the scene like a crescent moon. The trains rolling in, men breaking their backs under the weight of the heavy sacks. Harsh boots crunching on soft snow. A threat of violence in the air and a wooden hut billowing black smoke.

Throughout the months of November and December, frostbitten, charcoal memories form in Stephen's mind. 'Life', as he is careful to place in quotation marks, continues at the front. By design, there's not enough food. There is too much time spent performing hard, physical labour in the freezing, sub-zero conditions and too few opportunities to wash and rest. It doesn't take long before the camp is riddled with lice. Stephen always sleeps in his clothes. It's simply too cold, too dangerous to undress. Besides, he is frequently woken up abruptly, either for work or by soldiers bursting in to kick them all out when they need the house to themselves, for their 'love life', as Stephen writes sarcastically in one of his letters. Soldiers use the empty house to coerce women from the nearby village, forcing them to perform sexual acts, sometimes in exchange for a bit of food.

The soldiers come up with an array of crooked deals for their personal gain, exploiting both the villagers as well as the forced labourers. A rather lucrative side hustle develops, in which soldiers who are about to go on leave offer to post flimsy notes to forced labourers' loved ones as a sign of life in exchange for money. Stephen doesn't partake, not because he doesn't believe it would work, but because he is unmarried and doesn't have anyone to send a note to.

It's unlike Stephen to not want to send his mother a note, even if there is no guarantee that it would arrive. Perhaps, it must be pride preventing him from wanting to be a part of any of the soldiers' schemes. But there's a bitterness in his writing and a weary tone in the tape. Hungarian soldiers treating their own people this way leaves scars deeper than those of sticks against backs.

Dust settles on an unplayed piano. It creeps into its innards. When the layer grows thick enough, it dulls the impact of the hammer on string. The result: a muted sound. Like dust, the bitter cold, the smoke and the cruelty of his countrymen coat Stephen's thoughts. The hours of work, the humiliation, the lack of food, the poor sanitation – it all takes its toll.

After a short, but heavy sleep, Stephen wakes in a cold sweat. He tosses his flea-ridden blanket aside, causing the floorboards beneath him to shake as he turns to scratch a violent itch all over his shoulder. He hears angry shouts, ordering him to get to work. As the first train rolls in, Stephen's stomach tightens into a burning knot. Lifting the usual two sacks onto his back, he can feel the knot turning and his abdomen cramping. Pale-faced, he forces himself through the day, beads of sweat freezing on his skin as he jogs across the camp carrying cargo.

Stephen has dysentery, an infection of the intestines caused by contaminated food or water. He's seen what the soldiers do to those who slow down the work. Keeping his weakness concealed as best he can, he continues to heave the sacks through the snow. Stephen prays the supervisors won't notice and hopes no one else will tell on him, perhaps in the hope of putting themselves in a more favourable position. He hates this thought and tries pushing it out of his mind by concentrating on placing one foot in front of the other, balancing a sack of munitions over his shoulder. Soldiers' boots in the corners of his eyes, he focuses his gaze into the near distance, a vacant stare upon his pale, clammy face.

The train rolls out. It's still early afternoon and the sun is setting. An icy wind whips across Stephen's face. Droplets of snow cling to his beard where they crystallise, glistening in the harsh spotlight. Stephen rushes into the hut, others shuffle around, making room for him as he sits there, shivering violently. Between the men, he warms up quickly, but his eyes start to sting as the smoke from the fire assaults his face, permeating his clothes and clinging to the hairs in his nostrils.

Motioning out on to the clearing towards the growing wall of supplies, one of the older men says: 'It looks like a scene from one of those films, where the Egyptians built the Pyramids with Jewish slaves.'

'At least it was hot in Egypt,' Stephen replies drily.

A rare eruption of coarse laughter fills the shack. A familiar sensation akin to a warm electric current rushes through Stephen's body – it feels good to entertain, to make people laugh. His instinct is to laugh along too, but as he does, thick, black smoke clogs his throat and races into his lungs. He coughs violently.

Now everybody was equal, chased and hunted.

Stephen wakes to the deafening blow of a bomb. With a start, he jumps up from the floor and tries to make sense of the chaos unfolding around him. Gunshots, shouts in a multitude of languages, footsteps and the screech of a train. Stephen realises that his supervisors are panicking and retreating. The cruel bravado of their booming voices gone, he makes out nervous shouts of, 'They've broken through!', 'They've crossed the river!' And finally hears the order, 'Every man for themselves'.

A hand hoists Stephen by the collar of his coat, jolting him forwards and nearly knocking him off his feet. It's one of the men Stephen had become friendly with back in Transylvania, who's now broken into a run – away from the camp, towards the woods. Stephen catches his step, spins around to grab his rucksack, and follows him. Four others, Stephen can now see as he's sprinting, are about twenty metres ahead of them and have already reached the safety of the trees. They run as fast as they can without turning around to see what, if anything, is following them. Soon the soundtrack of gunshots and shouts fades and is replaced by the rising sound of their choked breathing and heavy footsteps. One by one they fall into a jog and then a brisk walk, before eventually daring to stop, just for a moment – bent backs and hands on knees, panting for breath and surveying their surroundings.

'What do we do?' says one, each word punctuated by heavy breathing.

'Surrender to the Russians?' another suggests.

'That's a terrible idea!' echo Stephen and the others.

In silent agreement that there is no other option, they strap their rucksacks on to a sledge and continue to walk.

On this Tuesday night of 13 January 1943, Stephen walks through the night. He knows exactly what day it is and commits it to memory. It is his mother's birthday.

The sun has set and there is no choice other than to keep walking so as not to freeze. *If it weren't for her sheepskin coat*, Stephen thinks, I would surely die.

CHAPTER 11

It's Either You or Me

What the cassette tapes lack in factual detail, they make up for in nuance, in the unsaid, in the implied. All the subtleties of Stephen's delivery, his Hungarian accent, the pauses he leaves before he concludes a thought, the silence assigning extra meaning to the last word of a sentence. His handwritten letters usually fill the factual gaps. They are rich with names, places, exact dates and contain a lot more of Stephen's inner thoughts and feelings. Neither tapes nor letters, though, give away his specific location in Russia, nor do they adequately portray the depths of his suffering. I am getting to know my grandfather rather well and am developing a strong sense for when he is omitting certain facts, the implications delicately dancing around his cadence. Whether it is to protect himself or those who love him, or a combination of the two, the sharpest edges are sanded down in his retelling. Still, Stephen is a storyteller and tends to artfully hint at unspoken depths. I recognise some of the same tricks I use in my telling – communicating uncomfortable truths in prose, allowing us to share it and to live, without letting it destroy us.

I research the painful details, deliberately omitted by my grandfather. Jewish forced labourers were exposed to grinding brutality at the front. Their suffering was often increased tenfold by the treatment they received at the hands of the Hungarian officers and soldiers in charge of them. Around 80 per cent of Jewish forced labourers never returned home, falling prey to battle, captivity, disease and outright murder committed by Hungarian soldiers.

From eyewitness accounts of other survivors, I learn some of the many horrific practices that took place at labour camps similar to the one my grandfather was at. Under the command of especially sadistic officers, Jewish slave labourers were subjected to so-called calisthenics and forced, for example, to do leapfrogs and somersaults after their eleven-hour shifts. The men were humiliated, beaten, tortured and murdered. Often they were made to replace horses that had collapsed or died of exhaustion. Some were made to pull heavily laden wagons to 'save the energy of the animals', whose lives were deemed more valuable than those of the Jews.

When I read these details, a sombreness falls upon my body. I know that Stephen must have suffered such abuse, even if he never reached a readiness to talk about it – it echoes in my bones. As any skilled storyteller would, he hints at unspoken atrocities, trusting the audience to fill in the blanks with their own imagination and feel the hurt coursing through their own consciousness.

The conditions under which the Hungarian labour servicemen lived and worked was especially brutal in the Ukraine and in Russia. This was down to the viciously antisemitic attitudes held by many of the guards and company commanders. Their behaviour did not only reflect their own attitudes, but also the instructions of their superiors back at home, not to mention the years of poisonous antisemitic propaganda they had all been exposed to in their daily lives. The treatment of the forced labourers was so horrendous that many intentionally surrendered to the Soviets after the breach and entered the prisoner-of-war system, thinking they couldn't be worse off there than with their own countrymen. The Soviets, of course, regarded the slave labourers as Hungarian soldiers and showed them no mercy. Only roughly a quarter of those who became prisoners of war survived.

After the breakthrough of the Soviet Army, some of the Jewish labourers were simply massacred by Hungarian forces. In Doroshevich, six hundred Jewish workers were locked in a barn and burnt alive – retreating soldiers having set the barn on fire. The official report stated that the fire was caused by the Jews themselves by smoking cigarettes.

Incidentally, Stephen writes in his letter, almost as an aside, *the corporal who was in charge of us has overdone his cruelty and was charged and sentenced after the war.*

Not many perpetrators actually faced consequences for their actions. I read of a Hungarian Lieutenant, Lipot Muray, who was sentenced to death for brutalities committed as commander of a Jewish labour battalion, and I wonder how likely it is that he might have been responsible for my grandfather's poor treatment. Whether he was or not, the fact remains that most of the Hungarian Jewish workers who died on the Eastern Front did so as the direct result of deliberately cruel or neglectful actions by Hungarian forces.

That's not to say that there weren't exceptions. Not all cogs oil the machine. General Vilmos Nagy became Hungary's Minister of Defence in September 1942 and was appalled to learn how Hungarian labour servicemen were being treated. After a visit to Hitler's headquarters near Vinnitsa, he issued a series of instructions in an attempt to evoke change. Those directives included that labour servicemen no longer be treated like prisoners of war, that the ill and aged be discharged, that food rations were to be improved to enable the men to work and that corporal punishment and maltreatment of any kind should stop with immediacy. The issue was that people stationed outside of Hungary simply paid no heed to his decree. Unsurprisingly, Nagy's attempt to change course was unpopular within the Hungarian government. He was ridiculed, accused of being a 'Jewish lackey' (Zsidóbérenc), and found himself under constant attack by the extreme political right, whose views by now well and truly outnumbered his. Within months, Nagy was replaced by a general more sympathetic to Germany. It's ironic that some of the most intense suffering occurred among the labour servicemen during Nagy's reign, which coincided with the Soviet breakthrough and was defined by the chaos that unfolded in its wake. No form of resistance, though, is futile. Every voice against hatred matters and is eventually heard. Nagy's actions were recognised. He became the first Hungarian to receive the 'Righteous Among the Nations' – an honorific used by the State of Israel to describe non-Jews who risked their lives during the Holocaust to save people from extermination by the Nazis.

Stephen's story weaves its way into my daily routine. I listen to him playing piano while I write. In my flat in London, I spend evenings staring at maps, looking up how long a train journey would take from Hungary to Russia, how many days it would take to walk from Stary Oskol to the River Don. For weeks, I'm preoccupied with finding out exactly where in Russia he was, so I decide to reread the chapter on forced labour in *The Politics of Genocide*. One particular sentence sends a jolt through my body: 'The sacrificial attrition of the labour service companies began in the wake of the Soviet break-through near Voronezh early in January 1943.'

I repeat out loud to myself, before excitedly shouting across the flat to my partner: 'He was in Voronezh!'

An idea strikes me and, when it does, I instantly feel like it should have occurred to me sooner. At my laptop, I open up a search window and type in the date, 13 January 1943, along with the simple search terms 'Russia' and 'WWII' to see if I can find any records of this fateful day in Stephen's story. Sure enough, there it is – the information waiting for me patiently: 13 January 1943: The 'Ostrogozhsk–Rossosh offensive'. Stephen witnessed the first of what was a three-phased military attack by the Soviet Army on the Eastern Front called the Voronezh–Kharkov offensive.

Unbeknownst to Stephen, Soviet soldiers were advancing daily by roughly ten kilometres, while he was slaving away at the camp. Once the Hungarian soldiers started retreating, Stephen and thousands of other Jewish forced labourers were simply abandoned, left to fend for themselves without food or other supplies in the Russian winter.

I read the following passage in my textbook:

In the chaos that followed the Voronezh debacle, many of the labour service companies simply disintegrated. The commanders and guards deserted their posts, leaving Jews either under the control of a handful of subordinates or to their own fate. The straggling labour servicemen, bundled in their lice-infested rags and blankets, were subjected to unbelievable humiliation and torture during the long retreat. With the logistics in disarray, they were deprived of even the meagre food rations they had received while their companies were still relatively intact. Occasionally, they were driven out of shelters by intruding German or Hungarian soldiers; they felt compelled to walk throughout the night to avoid freezing to death. Emaciated by hunger and numbing cold and infested with lice, many of the labour servicemen who survived the debacle and escaped or avoided capture by the Red Army succumbed to a variety of diseases. In the absence of hospital facilities or medication, many of these died by the wayside.

It gives me a strange mix of sadness and satisfaction to learn that my grandfather's story is so representative of this part of our collective history.

Stephen grows weaker. His condition worsens and he is forced to walk slower – to take brief, but increasingly frequent, rests. As he trudges through snow-covered, tree-lined fields, the five men ahead of him go in and out of focus. His vision is blurring with exhaustion. He stops, leans forward and rests his gloved hands on his knees. Thick clouds of air form around his face as he breathes heavily. He looks up to see that his companions have stopped too. After looking back at Stephen, they huddle together in hushed conversation. After what feels like an awkwardly lengthy moment of flickering of eyes, nudging, gesticulating and more whispering, one of the men slowly approaches Stephen. The nominated spokesperson leans forward to meet Stephen's eyes.

'Istvan, I'm sorry . . . you're slowing us down too much.' The words hang in the air.

Stephen is rooted to the spot. There is complete silence, save for his heavy breathing and the diminishing crunch of the men's footsteps ahead. He watches as five silhouettes shrink further and further towards the grey, snow-covered horizon until they finally disappear.

Exactly what words were exchanged and how they were taken remains guesswork aided by subtext and tone. In his letter, Stephen calls these men his 'friends', framing the word in bitter parentheses. In the cassette tapes, his words are spoken with a cool sarcasm as he describes how they 'had a little conference' before telling him he was slowing them down too much. Suddenly the absence of their names strikes me. Stephen's retelling is rich with names, but the 'friends' he made in the labour camp, save for Laslo, remain anonymous. It is as though he erased them from his memory as a consequence of their betrayal. I turn my thoughts inward, trying to feel what he must have felt in that moment, but for the first time, I'm struggling to do so. As I'm trying to focus, I hear those ominous opening chords of 'An Old Mill is Dreaming' in my mind. They suddenly sound like laboured, heavy footsteps trudging through snow. And then I remember how it felt to hear his voice for the very first time: that deep Hungarian accent describing his song with the ghost piano whirling around in the background: the old mill 'stood alone, deserted'.

Stephen forces himself to keep walking. Alone, he trudges through the snowfields. He walks for a slow and laboured six to eight hours before he feels his rucksack getting heavy. It pulls his weakened shoulders backward, each step now requiring increased effort. An internal monologue begins, in which he weighs up the pros and cons of discarding his worldly belongings. Somewhere on the snow-covered ground between Voronezh and the Ukrainian border, Stephen stops.

I'm not going to sacrifice my life for my belongings, he thinks, and dumps his rucksack on the ground. He turns to face it, standing perfectly still. He opens his mouth to speak and as the words leave Stephen's chapped lips, they gather in an icy cloud, before vanishing into the cold air: 'It's either you or me!'

CHAPTER 12

Everybody's Prey

I was determined to get back to Hungary.

Circumstance has a firm hold, but the soul is unconquerable. I have always felt within me a great deal of determination. I used to think it was aided by youthful naivety – that not knowing how firmly the odds are stacked against me is what allows me to take on the world, all confident and headstrong. But my dad proved me wrong. He was full of beautiful resolve, even in the face of knowing too much. Resolve sits deep within us. Even when the odds are clear, we try.

Stephen is determined to continue on foot for as long as he can. As he walks, powerful emotions assault his tired body – fresh waves of anger, a wash of loneliness and momentary flickers of panic. The severity of his situation sets with the sun. The temperature drops to a deadly minus forty-two degrees, an oddly specific number that Stephen mentions in the tapes. The snow-covered field surrounding him grows dark and, in the absence of light, the silence grows louder, heightening his senses and piercing his thoughts. One certainty crystallises in Stephen's mind – he doesn't want to walk through another night. He is going to have to find shelter, or else he will surely freeze.

Like a rising melody, determination fights its way through fear. Stephen composes with the only sounds ushering into the night: the icy air escaping his lungs slowly matching the rhythm of his footsteps. A meditative state befalls him. For the first time since the setting of the sun, he notices that the sky above is clear and full of stars. Isn't it quintessentially human to call upon forces greater than ourselves in moments of need? Lost, Stephen starts to pray. After all, he thinks, there is something rather biblical about the scene: the dark, winter night and himself, the only moving silhouette under the starlit sky, guided by their dulled light.

Dusk came and I was lost – I was lost – there was nothing but snow, snow and snow and me, all by myself, in the middle of it. So I prayed to God for some guidance and, as if he heard my prayer, suddenly in the distance, there was a light *flickering.*

His accent places the emphasis on the penultimate word. Invigorated by the vision, Stephen quickens his pace towards the light up ahead. In the distance he makes out the shadow of trees. As he trudges closer, he sees the trees are framing a path, at the end of which the light he is following flickers more brightly. The wave of excitement is interrupted by a thought: whoever is behind it is likely not an empathetic soul. Hesitation lasts a mere moment, a pang of doubt rushing down his spine before it evaporates. He continues his steps in the knowledge that there is no other choice to be made, other than to trust.

The light, Stephen can now make out, is coming from behind the windows of a small farmhouse at the junction of the path. Proceeding with caution, he chooses the stable over the front door. With a stiff, gloved hand, Stephen lifts the latch on the iron door and carefully pulls it open. A sigh of relief escapes his frozen lungs as he finds himself alone, save for a shaggy-haired horse in the far corner, who seems utterly unperturbed by Stephen's presence. Trying to make as little sound as possible, he buries himself in the hay for warmth and falls into a short, deep asleep.

When Stephen awakes, he thinks it wise to try to remain undetected and continues on foot before sunrise. Without a soul to speak to, his inner monologue grows stronger. As he walks, he begins to bargain with himself, finally promising that he'll walk no further than up until midday, so that he will have enough time to find shelter – a safe place to rest – before dusk, when temperatures drop to the unbearable.

True to his word, Stephen holds to this routine. For weeks, he walks roughly twenty kilometres each day and seeks refuge before the setting of the sun. But for the first time since I set out to explore and share Stephen's story, history books don't follow his tracks. This lonely walk through Russia is a story unique to my grandfather and just a handful of others, whose versions of events have largely been lost in time. All I have are the cassette recordings. Now, it's just the two of us – Stephen telling his story and me, hanging on his every word.

There's a long pause on the tape. All I can hear is the loud static, as if I'm listening to Stephen trying to think. Finally, his voice reappears in a solemn conclusion:

That was very deadly what happened to me . . . to be left alone. I wouldn't want to do that again.

On good days, he sleeps in stables and pigsties, as they provide the best source of warmth. Besides, as Stephen states matter-of-factly, with his deteriorating appearance, he 'belonged there'. With no chance to wash, the daily grime clings to his one set of clothes and his lice- and frostbitten skin. His dark hair and ginger beard grow long and wild, hiding his delicate features from the cold. Stephen avoids starvation by eating scraps he finds in the stables and pigsties – mostly rotting potatoes and onion peelings. Occasionally, strangers help him by offering him a crust of bread or fresh vegetable scraps. He's quick to learn that the poorer the people, the more likely they are to show him kindness. Stephen's homebound path is neither the fastest nor the most direct route. He zig-zags the land, initially skirting around the more populated areas, occasionally asking a stranger for directions when it feels safe to do so, to make sure he's heading west.

To fend off the cold and to distract himself from feelings of nausea and his aching abdomen, Stephen imagines himself elsewhere. As he walks, instead of in this wintry no-man's-land, he's back in London and trudging down Oxford Circus selling scarves to wholesalers. On other occasions, he pictures the Danube River on his left, and he's strolling down Budapest's promenade after a late show at The Dunacorzo. To measure time, Stephen runs through pieces of music in his mind – twice around his usual dinnertime performance sees him roughly through from sunrise to noon, at which point he knows to start keeping an eye out for shelter. It suddenly strikes me that this is a habit of mine – using music to measure time. It is a trick my dad taught me when I was little. On lengthy car journeys, of which there were many, the two of us would sometimes sing through albums we knew and loved to pass the time (it takes thirty-three minutes and fifty-five seconds to sing The Beatles *Help!* album, if you sing at the correct tempo). What if this characteristic originated here, in Stephen's snowy isolation? What if my father learned it from his?

Faces appear before him. One, in particular, accompanies Stephen. When he thinks of Roszi, his heart sinks. The profundity of the heartache he feels pulls his focus into view. It shifts his thoughts towards Budapest, towards coming home. He envisions himself walking through the front door of his parents' apartment, reuniting with them and the piano. A warmth fills him, allowing him to quicken his step.

But then, a different kind of chill befalls him. Even in the joyous event of his own return, others will surely be less fortunate.

Laslo Somogyi's whereabouts occupy Stephen's mind. In the tapes, his name comes up frequently – far more than those of his siblings and closest friends. He interrupts his own flow of storytelling, taking a sharp and unexpected detour, theorising on what fate may have befallen his bad-weather friend. He wonders whether he may have given himself up to the Russians. Some, he says, had planned to do so in hushed conversations back in the labour camps. Stephen thinks that there's no chance anyone could make it back to Hungary by heading east, but admittedly, at this moment in time, even his ambitions of returning seem just as impossible a dream.

Every day, my little twenty kilometres. March set in and I was still walking . . .

Unbeknownst to Stephen, the Russian Army is advancing at the same pace, roughly twenty kilometres a day. Even with his deviations, he manages to keep a relatively safe distance. The Soviets, though, are by no stretch the only danger facing Stephen. The deadliest and most acute of dangers are the arctic temperatures and the cruel isolation, but Stephen is now a fugitive – every encounter carries with it a great risk. He is on the run from the Russian, German and Hungarian armies, and to those who cross his path, he is an unwelcome intruder at best. With an aching, hollow stomach and a light-headedness, Stephen has to weigh up the risk before begging for food.

I was everybody's prey – everybody was against me. Anybody could have killed me on the road with no consequences at all.

In April, the scenery surrounding Stephen slowly turns from rural, snow-covered wasteland to a more populated suburbia. For the first time, he braves a direct route – walking through the small village before him, rather than wasting time and energy navigating around it. As he shuffles his bedraggled body down the high street, children stop and point at him. 'The devil! The devil!' they shout.

If Stephen had a mirror, he too would be frightened by his own reflection. Much like the emaciated, dark figure walking down the street, the increasingly urban landscapes surrounding Stephen are a husk of their former selves. As he walks, he passes bombed-out buildings, destroyed streets and abandoned homes.

He kicks a piece of rubble out of his way and hears a familiar sound; a memory of home rushes through Stephen's body as he over-hears fragments of Hungarian. He's quick to remember, however, that running into fellow countrymen, these days, does not always mean safety, and tempers his excitement. Only when he turns to see that the voices are coming from similarly bedraggled characters, does he dare make contact.

'Servus.' A tentative greeting escapes his lips as he remembers that he hasn't spoken out loud to anyone for days. For the first time in a while, Stephen's words meet empathetic ears.

'Jó napot bátyám!' (Good day, my brother!) one of the men replies, his voice coarse but warm and containing an element of surprise at stumbling across yet another Hungarian serviceman. They exchange names and brief stories. Soon, the small group of stragglers walk together, finally reaching their shelter for the night: a bombed-out train station on the outskirts of Kyiv in modern-day Ukraine.

Stephen is no longer alone and with that realisation, he drops to his knees. With one quick motion, he pulls his mother's gold chain from around his neck, rolls it into a ball and stuffs it between tooth and cheek, before losing consciousness.

CHAPTER 13

How the Chances Are Happening

'*A bombed-out train station on the outskirts of Kyiv . . .*'
As I'm writing this, the world has just passed a grim anniversary of Russia's invasion of Ukraine. I see footage of bombed-out Kyiv every day on the news. It fills me with an ancient sadness. I feel Stephen's despair at the thought of war, again, in Europe.

The Germans invaded Ukraine in June 1941, nineteen months prior to Stephen arriving there. At first, the Germans were largely welcomed with open arms, the Ukrainians thinking that allyship would help them gain independence. That thinking was quickly proven wrong. Within days, the organisers of Ukraine's independence movement were arrested and put in concentration camps. Cultural activities were repressed, and education was limited to a primary-school level. The Nazis also implemented their 'racial' policies. Stephen comments on how there used to be many Jews in Ukraine, but they were all killed by the Germans. He commits to tape a rare gruesome detail – Jews being lined up, forced to strip naked and dig their own graves, in which they would then be shot. In total, an estimated 1.5 million Ukrainian Jews were murdered, and over eight hundred thousand were displaced.

Stephen is in Kyiv at a time of heightened tension. With the Russian army approaching, an eerie chaos hangs heavy in the air.

Soon, German soldiers will begin their slow retreat from Ukraine, leaving wholesale destruction in their wake.

We don't experience time in a linear way. Often, it forebodes and replays; it creeps up on us and takes us by surprise. Sometimes, it stands still. I'm sure I was small this morning. I have such a strong memory of sitting next to my mother on public transport, staring down at my skinny little legs and thinking: *Remember this! One day you'll want to look back on how your feet couldn't even reach the ground.*

And here I am, exactly the same age as Stephen is as he lies unconscious on the floor of a bombed-out station in Kyiv.

Stephen's experience, with all its sombre emotion, will inevitably spill on to his children. I may not have history books to corroborate this part of Stephen's story, but I do have the accounts of my dad and my aunt. What is a song, if not a truth passed down through generations? Sometimes, the melody is dark.

'Does he mention witnessing soldiers rape a woman?' Julie asks me, as we're sat on the sofa together. The question catches me off-guard. I hesitate for a moment, mentally replaying this chapter of Stephen's story in my mind. I conclude that he hadn't and ask her to elaborate.

Julie tells me that her father at some point confessed to her that, one day as he was hiding in a bombed-out station in Kyiv, he saw a group of German soldiers corner and rape a woman. Of course, had he intervened, it would have most certainly meant his own death. The guilt clung to him for the rest of his life.

When my dad and Julie were little, Stephen would tell them bedtime stories: tales of a man who walked through the Russian winter, a winter so cold that the only way to survive was to never stop moving. In these bedtime stories, Stephen tells his children how he walked past corpses of men who had pulled down their trousers to 'do their business' and had instantly frozen to death.

This image would dance before my dad's closed eyes as he tried, and failed, to fall asleep. As children, Richard and Julie found their father's stories terrifying and terrific in equal measure. To them, Stephen was a hero worthy of their childhood books – 'strong as an ox', all muscular and red-bearded, battling against all odds. With these bedtime stories of survival, a thin layer of helplessness and guilt starts to build within them. Throughout their childhood and well into their adult lives, they would struggle with feeling both unworthy and under the shadow of their father's hurt.

Stephen comes to. The clear sky above him shifts in and out of focus as he realises he's alive and still lying on the floor of the bombed-out station. The others notice him stirring and one of them rushes to kneel beside him, a cup of milk at the ready.

'Istvan! Friend, I'm glad to see you awake!'

It takes Stephen a great deal of strength to prop himself up and to open his mouth to speak. Before he has a chance to ask the question on his mind, the answer is given by the man at his side: 'We were worried – you've been in and out of consciousness for nearly two weeks now.

'Listen,' he continues, in an oddly nonchalant and conversational tone for someone speaking to a man so close to his premature death. 'More have joined – there are about fifty of us now! So many are injured . . . We're staying here in the station house until we can get some help or are strong enough to continue.'

Stephen's surroundings remain a blur. Too much of his energy goes on staying awake. Every now and then, a fellow forced labourer comes to check on him and to replenish his cup of milk. For the majority of the day, though, he sits still, alone and in a daze. Suddenly he feels an urge to move. He crawls out of the station house and on to the deserted street. There, he sees a brick well. On all fours, he crawls towards it. As he reaches the well, Stephen peers over the side of it and sees a metal bucket floating on a small pool of dark water. Stephen looks around to ensure he's still unobserved and then grabs the rope and starts to pull. A pain shoots along his arms. Fighting through it, he manages to heave the bucket halfway up the well, before giving up and letting it crash onto the murky liquid. Exhausted, but not displeased with himself, he crawls back into the station house and collapses with a heavy sigh on to the ground. Every day, Stephen follows this secret routine: crawling out to the well, trying his strength and returning to rest. With every pull, he feels a little closer to his former self.

Of course that was my secret; I never told anybody, so that they wouldn't use me for something else which I didn't like!

Stephen keeps to himself, fearful of being put to work if the wrong person were to catch on to him regaining his strength. His spirit may be willing, but Stephen's body is fighting a serious battle. On top of the dysentery, Stephen, like so many thousands of other forced labourers, has caught typhoid fever. If untreated, this bacterial infection brings with it a host of medical complications.

Stephen is by no means the only one among the men in serious need of medical attention. Some are unconscious, as he had been. Others are wounded and lie motionless. Many are delirious – shouting and cursing at invisible foes or begging to be relieved of their lives. Stephen, too, starts to hallucinate. He has moments in semi-consciousness where he's convinced he's back in Budapest, that all he has to do is walk down one more street before he's finally home. One such second of delirium is interrupted by a Russian plane flying overhead – a sudden and brutal reminder of his current reality.

As he exhales loudly after another stint at the well, the same unnamed man appears before Stephen: 'Hey! There's a Hungarian soldier here with us.'

Stephen turns his head in alarm.

'No, it's okay – we're being evacuated! He wants to take us to a military hospital here in Kyiv so we can rest and then continue on home. It's not far – are you okay to walk?'

By now, there are nearly two hundred of them assembled at the bombed-out station. Those who are able to walk unaided, Stephen among them, are grouped together by one of the soldiers and assigned a number, which makes him feel deeply uncomfortable. The memory of what happened the last time he was randomly assigned a number sends a pang of anger through his aching body. But he feels he has no choice other than to swallow his feelings and submit in the hope that this is the way to get home.

Despite his reservations, Stephen is quick to notice that the soldier leading them into Kyiv is entirely different in demeanour and seems serious about providing them with care. It is nothing but the luck of the draw. At this moment in time, General Vilmos Nagy is still Hungary's Minister of Defence and has sent orders to round up and bring home all Hungarian soldiers, including forced labourers. A command by an unpopular leader is seldom fulfilled and Nagy's anti-racist commands fell on many deaf ears.

The men reach the military hospital, but are refused entry. The commanding officer stationed there won't allow Jews in under his watch. The hospital is for soldiers only; this is his final word. On the tapes, Stephen's tone is bitter as he recounts how they were refused medical help because they weren't 'pure blood', his voice placing angry quotation marks around those words.

Instead, Stephen and the other men in his group are led to an abandoned, bombed-out school on the opposite side of the square. It is poorly equipped, but there are some basics such as stretchers and rudimentary medical supplies sent by the Red Cross. There are no doctors or nurses on hand to take care of forced labourers. However, there is a doctor in their number. It's thanks to him that Stephen finally receives some desperately needed medical attention.

I contained water in my body and, as a consequence, I was swelling up. Of course, it was my heart, which couldn't function very well.

My dad's legs started to swell up a couple of weeks before he died. Those were the days of the most extreme cognitive dissonance. With Stephen's words, I feel every molecule in my body jolt right back into position, reliving the moment I first noticed Dad's swollen ankles straining against stretched jeans. Those were also the days of the most intense feelings. We squeezed every drop of love and joy out of them.

'What would you prefer your life to be?' my dad once asked me. I was a teenager and deeply upset over one thing or another. I had been inconsolable, but my dad had such a special way of reaching me with his kind pragmatism.

'Would you rather your life were like a flat field: pleasant, but uneventful and predictable?'

I raised my head from my hands and turned to look up at him inquisitively.

'Or would you rather have your life be like a cityscape, with an exciting skyline full of ups and downs?'

I have never stopped thinking about that metaphor.

*   *   *

The fresh wave of anger and disappointment at being refused help subsides as Stephen rests his head on a stretcher in the makeshift medical facility. He's simply too exhausted to dwell on the setback. Instead, he focuses on the sounds around him: the hushed voices of the many men around him, a horse-drawn cart somewhere out in the square and more Russian planes overhead. His fever spikes and he once again slips in and out of consciousness. He has the same recurring vision:

I had dreams of being at home – that I would just have to walk down one more road and I'd be at my parents' house. Of course it was a bitter disappointment that, instead of home, I was in a school in Kyiv.

With rest and medication, Stephen's health improves along with the weather. It's April, and Stephen once again creates his own routine to aid his recovery. Every day, he gets up and walks around the school's courtyard to measure his strength, much like he had done with the bucket in the well. Mostly, though, he rests and falls in and out of sleep throughout the day. One particularly light sleep is interrupted as the same soldier who escorted them to the school comes running into the building, shouting into the room for all who are well enough to hear that a train has arrived and that the station manager is sending carriages to come and collect them.

'We're going home – if you have belongings, get them packed!' he shouts triumphantly as he turns on his heel and heads back out to the square to wait for the carriages.

In that moment, the fever dream becomes real. Stephen, for the first time in months, feels a deep sense of relief wash over him. Elated, he decides to take one more walk around the school. That day, he hardly feels the tightness in his limbs as he walks.

He hears them before he sees them: a glorious medley of hooves trotting on cobblestones and screeching wheels coming to a halt. At first, he's excited as he sees a commanding officer approach the courtyard, several horse-drawn coaches trailing behind him. Stephen watches as he's greeted by the soldier supervising the school. He's not close enough to overhear the conversation, but the soldier's raised voice and flailing arms do not bode well. Something is not going to plan. Stephen moves a little closer, although he daren't approach them fully, as he watches the commanding officer turn away from the soldier and march in the opposite direction, towards the military hospital. A sinking yet familiar feeling sets in as Stephen realises what's happening: the orders are strictly to bring back Hungarian soldiers, not forced labourers, or at least that's how this particular commanding officer is choosing to interpret them. There's nothing left for Stephen to do other than to watch his ticket home slip away as the half-empty coaches and that particular train home leaves for Budapest without him.

I pause the tape. Before I continue listening to Stephen's story, I take a minute to let myself feel the rage that Stephen so elegantly omits in his retelling. I sit in silence and think on how terrifyingly easy it is to poison humans against one another. How little time it takes to erode a person's empathy and fill them instead with fear. Whether the commanding officer was simply covering his own back or whether he genuinely believed himself superior to my grandfather and the other men in the school is irrelevant. In this moment, the power lay with him. I press play and continue listening to my grandfather. As if he somehow knows I need consoling, his tone shifts. The bitter disappointment in his voice is gone, replaced with an air of anticipation. With the first sentence, I'm instantly drawn back into his story:

Now. How the chances are happening in this life . . . I will tell you, how I got out.

CHAPTER 14

The Piano Player of Budapest

Unsure which emotion to bow to, Stephen stays rooted to the spot. He stands perfectly still long after the last echo of hooves on cobblestones has vanished into the distance. He watches the soldier kick a piece of rubble in frustration and sink on to a bench in the courtyard. He can't bear the thought of going back into the school, of lying down on the same stretcher again. Instead he decides to walk around the courtyard once more, for no reason other than not knowing what else to do. He places one foot in front of the other mindlessly and circles the courtyard. Then, still not ready to retreat into the school, he walks around the makeshift medical facility. Before he knows it, he's back where he started. He notices the soldier is still sitting on the bench, staring out into the distance. The soldier's gaze, though, now falls on a uniformed man turning off from the main road into the courtyard. Stephen can tell, by the soldier's reaction, that this is an unexpected visit. The uniformed man addresses the soldier, who promptly springs to his feet. Stephen is equally as desperate to overhear as he is to remain undetected, so he inches forward with caution.

He hears the unexpected officer ask: 'Any Hungarians left here? I have a train heading back to Debrecen.'

Disheartened by the recent rejections, the soldier replies: 'No, no soldiers left – only servicemen – about two hundred of them, actually, there in the school.'

As the commanding officer's gaze follows the soldier's arm, somewhat lazily gesturing towards the school behind him, he sees Stephen and, for a brief moment, their eyes meet.

'Well,' he says, as he shifts his gaze back to the soldier standing in front of him, 'they are Hungarians, are they not?'

The scene before Stephen seems to slow: the two men continue to converse, they nod and the soldier turns to march towards the school, giving Stephen a small, encouraging nod as he passes as if to say: *This time it's for real.* The unexpected visitor walks in the opposite direction, leaving the courtyard to call for coaches. Stephen worries that this plan too will fall through, that the coaches won't come. But after a short while, he hears the same song of horseshoes on cobblestones and he, along with the other men recovering in the bombed-out school, climb into the coaches and make their way to the train station.

Sat in the carriage together with their supervising soldier, Stephen learns just how much of a lucky break (or a 'helping hand from God', as he would call it) the arrival of this unexpected officer is: the train they were heading towards wasn't ever even meant to stop in Kyiv. It had been re-routed, the railway lines further south damaged by landmines. Arriving in Ukraine's capital, the commanding officer (Stephen doesn't remember his rank and refers to him sometimes as a commander, sometimes as a lieutenant), took it upon himself to find the military hospital to see if, now that he was here anyway, there were any Hungarians he could help home.

They arrive at the station. Stephen is queuing to board the train. The commanding officer stands inside the vestibule, keeping track of how many men are boarding. Stephen climbs into the carriage and, once again, their eyes meet.

'Wait.' He stops Stephen in his tracks with an intense, searching stare.

'Excuse me, aren't you Istvan Bastyai? The piano player of Budapest?'

Stephen is dumbfounded. With his shaved head and filthy, over-sized red shirt drowning his dangerously thin frame, he doesn't understand how anyone could recognise him.

'Yes,' he replies with hesitant bewilderment, 'yes, I am.'

A broad smile fills the commander's face. 'This is incredible!' he says, failing to contain his excitement. With the flat side of a curled-up fist, he punches the side of the carriage door, as an expression of his disbelief.

'Don't you remember me?' He looks at Stephen expectantly.

'No, I'm . . . I'm sorry.' Stephen is exhausted and, as anyone would be in this situation, a little embarrassed.

It's frustratingly difficult to make out the man's name on the cassette tapes. My best guess by listening to the tapes over and over and looking up Hungarian first and last names, is that he is called Zerind Wali. Zerind, as he reminds Stephen, is a fellow Hungarian musician. He and Stephen had played together on the same circuit of clubs and restaurants before the war broke out. Apparently, the music industry is as small as the odds of this encounter.

'I'm so happy I found you,' he says.

Then he asks Stephen, somewhat foolishly, 'Have you done much playing lately?'

'No, actually, I've just been doing a lot of walking,' Stephen replies, his Hungarian sense of humour as sharp as the collar bones poking out from underneath his neck.

'There's an upright piano in the front carriage! You simply must come and play for us! Have a seat, we'll get going and at some point I'll come and call for you, okay?'

Stephen initially protests, fearing his fingers and heart may be too weak to play, but finally agrees when Zerind makes it clear that there is also an abundance of red wine, to which he would be welcome, if he consents to give them a concert.

Stephen takes a seat. He watches the other men climb on to the train and shuffle past him. Finally, the train doors close and, with a jolt, it springs forward. *I'm on my way home.* He allows the thought to sink in. Still in disbelief at the encounter, at being recognised in the state he's in, Stephen turns his thoughts to the prospect of having to perform and suddenly feels nervous. He realises that it's been well over half a year since he's touched an instrument. This, he concludes, is by far the longest stretch of time he's ever gone without playing the piano. How strange, he thinks, that his returning home should be marked with this early reunion with a piano. Deep in thought, he hardly notices the hours pass. Soon, Zerind pokes his head into the carriage and calls for Stephen. Still full of excitement, he bounces through the train, leading him towards the two front carriages. The space is filled with uniformed officers sat in polite anticipation. Zerind guides him to the little upright piano.

Nervously, Stephen takes a seat and lifts the lid. He feels a strange confrontation with his former self, the black and white keys before him a brutal reminder of how far cruel circumstance has derailed him from his life and his music. After a brief moment of silence, Stephen drapes his hands over the keys and plays a long, flowery scale to test the tuning and sound of the instrument. Midway, his fingers stumble. He leans over to Zerind and whispers sheepishly: 'My hands aren't in good shape.'

'Oh, it doesn't matter . . . Play, play!' he says encouragingly, but slightly dismissively, with a booming voice. Everyone on the train has experienced war, but not everyone has endured what Stephen has. Zerind is not to know of Stephen's arduous journey on foot, nor of the extent of the abuse he suffered at the hands of Hungarian soldiers. And so he motions for Stephen to turn around and to continue playing: 'Come on, have a drink!'

Zerind gestures towards a barrel of red wine, placed next to the upright piano. He grabs the rubber tube protruding from it and places the other end in Stephen's mouth. Stephen takes a couple of large sips. The wine helps and, after the rusty start, a combination of muscle memory and emotion take over.

Music is such a powerful force. It has the ability to change the energy of a space, to fill cold hearts with empathy and to remind us of what it is to be human. For a moment, Stephen feels weary and anxious of performing for a group of soldiers wearing the same uniform and likely sharing similar attitudes to those who abused him at the frontline. But as he plays, he is back where he belongs, lost in the sound, entertaining a grateful crowd. It is bliss.

Identity is a shapeshifter, bending to time, place and circumstance. To some of the men sat on either side of him, Stephen, just a couple of days ago, will have been a Jew first and foremost – a traitor, deserving of the abuse they were so readily shelling out. In this moment, though, they are not concerned with his rank – soldier or labour serviceman – or what tortures he has suffered. To those in the carriage, Stephen's identity is once again that of a piano player, providing a joyous soundtrack to their journey home. Growing in confidence, he dives into a medley of compositions. His own and all-time favourites flow as easily as the wine, into the hearts of those passengers in the first two carriages.

For a performer, timing is everything. A great musician knows when to bring the melody 'home'. After about forty-five minutes' joy, Stephen instinctively knows that he can play no more, that it is time to end the piece. This is much to the dismay of his audience, but after a short protest, Zerind leads the large round of applause and proclaims: 'Okay, everyone, let's all go and get some sleep.'

Stephen, Zerind and the rest of the audience slowly disperse, filing out of the front carriage and further down the train. A soldier offers to accompany Stephen back to his compartment. Just as he bids Stephen goodnight, there's an intensely loud explosion. Stephen instinctively covers his head as bags fall from the luggage compartment.

The whole train shook and nobody knew what had happened.

They've come to a sudden halt. Stephen opens his eyes and looks around, exchanging panicked glances with those beside him. For what feels like an eternity – about twenty minutes in reality – they sit in silence, waiting. They daren't move for fear of what may have caused the explosion. Finally, a soldier enters the carriage and informs them: 'We've hit a landmine. We're going to have to stay put until the damage is repaired.'

'Is anybody hurt?' a man asks the soldier.

'Not seriously – we're taking care of a few men with minor injuries. The two front carriages are completely destroyed, but there wasn't anybody in them, so luckily no fatalities.'

Stephen sits in a trance as he processes what he's just heard, the phrases 'two front carriages' and 'completely destroyed' ricocheting in his mind. Everything in those carriages – including the piano at which he had been sitting just a couple of minutes before – is gone, smashed completely. He thinks back on how strongly he felt it was time to stop playing. His former self would never have succumbed to tiredness. At Hotel Central he had insisted that it be included in his contract that, if he wanted to, he could play throughout the night. The irony that in this instance it was his own physical limitations that saved his life strikes him. And then he wonders – was it tiredness he felt in his bones that led him to stop playing? *Timing*, he thinks to himself as he sits there in a daze, *is everything*.

Eventually, they are able to continue their journey. In the early hours of the morning, they pull in to a station in the south of Poland for a short break before continuing onwards to Hungary. From his seat, Stephen looks out of the window and spies on the opposite platform the very same Red Cross train that had taken the Hungarian soldiers from Kyiv's military hospital; now it looks eerily empty and dark. Stephen steps out on to the platform to stretch his legs, but also to investigate the empty train. He approaches a guard who's leaning leisurely against one of the empty carriages.

'Excuse me, sir.' The guard looks up at Stephen. 'Do you know what happened to all the patients on this train? The Hungarian soldiers?'

'Oh,' the guard raises his eyebrows, clearly surprised at the question, 'they have been checked in to a military hospital.' He points along the length of the deserted platform. 'This was our end destination.'

What follows is an awkward moment of silence whereby the guard stares at Stephen, slightly perplexed as to why this information seems to have confused him. The guard watches the frail figure before him run through a sequence of thoughts in his mind before hesitantly interrupting: 'Can I help you with anything?'

'No . . . thank you.' Stephen gives an awkward wave and turns back to his train.

As he boards and climbs back onto his seat, he thinks on how the misfortune of not being allowed on that first train turned out not to be a misfortune at all. The Red Cross train was never going to Budapest. The train that Stephen was on, the one that wasn't supposed to go through Kyiv and wasn't supposed to bring home forced labourers, was heading to Hungary, minus the first carriages, but with my grandfather on board. Later, Stephen will hear rumours that the Hungarian soldiers in the Polish military hospital were soon taken as prisoners of war by the Russian army.

As they cross the Hungarian border, Stephen lets out a slow sigh of relief. He hadn't realised how tense he had been until he exhales and notices the whites of his knuckles. He unclenches his sweaty hands, which have been holding on tightly to the edge of his seat. The train finally pulls in to Debrecen, a midsize town in the north-east of Hungary. They disembark and are led to a facility where the men wash, de-louse and receive a change of clothes. From here, soldiers organise coaches to take the men back to Budapest's military hospital. The twists and turns of our own lives often rival those of fiction. As Stephen steps on to the bus, he notices a large poster on the partition between the driver and the passengers advertising the film *Help, I Inherited! (Segítség, örököltem!)'*. His name, Istvan Bastyai, is written in large, bold typeface.

How the chances are happening in this life . . .

It is October 1943 by the time Stephen arrives at the military hospital in Budapest. He weighs in at just forty-two kilos, having lost half his body weight during the three-month journey on foot. Stephen estimates that he walked 1,500km through the Russian winter, from where he was left to die to where he finally collapsed on the outskirts of Kyiv. Out of the 1,070 Jewish men drafted on this suicide mission to the frontline, he is one of only eight who returned – one for every note of the scale.

CHAPTER 15

Darker Clouds on the Horizon

*D*ue *to the strain and effort I made to stay alive I had lost a lot of weight. It took some time to regain those kilos.*

Stephen had held on so tightly to the thought of coming home during his walk through Russia. The carefully crafted, imagined return, one in which he would arrive on foot at his parents' doorstep, now seems naive in the harsh, flickering light of the military hospital. The coach had taken the men directly to it. Here, Stephen receives medical treatment and much-needed rest. It will take him months to regain his strength. The one delicious thought he holds on to as he recuperates is that his immediate family are alive and well. He is assured of this by the authorities shortly after he arrives and is told that they in turn have been notified of his survival. He is not permitted visitors, but the knowledge that his parents and sister are fine is the most effective of medicines.

Katica may not be allowed inside, but she comes to visit her son almost every day. From the street, she looks up at him through the glass window and waves. What a strange assortment of emotions this reunion must have brought with it. Katica will have been equally as overjoyed at the news of her firstborn's return as she would have been shocked at the sight of his skeletal frame.

For Katica and Aladar, the past year has been defined by both heart-wrenching goodbyes and tearful reunions with their sons. A couple of months prior to Stephen's return, Katica, Aladar and Annie were overjoyed to be able to meet Lorant at South Buda train station upon his early return from Ukraine.

Lorant has had a very different experience to Stephen. His saving grace was that he had fulfilled his mandatory conscription and joined the army early on. Somehow recognised as part of the machine, Lorant, unlike his brother, did not receive the same mistreatment and discrimination. When I first read Lorant's account of his time in the army serving in Ukraine, it strikes me as odd. Why would one brother be treated as a Hungarian and the other as a Jew? It is a good example of just how, by definition, a system that groups humans into separate races will be flawed and nonsensical.

Lorant, too, spends time in hospital, but makes a swift and full recovery. It is decided that he and the men from his unit sent back to recoup should not be returned to the war front in Ukraine and Russia. Instead, Lorant is sent to work on Budapest's newly built airport, Ferihegy, as is his younger brother, George. While this too is forced labour, Lorant and George are permitted to leave the site at night, to go home to their parents, as long as they are back at the barracks before sunrise.

The real reunion, after Stephen is discharged and the family is together again, even if just under cover of night, goes unrecorded in the tapes and remains a private moment between them.

I must tell you about an incident which was also not only significant but very rare.

Wearing his finest double-breasted suit and a stylish tweed over-coat, Stephen arrives at the administration office, stationed in a village on the outskirts of Budapest. Shortly after his discharge from hospital, he received a letter with an appointment in order to organise his release from the Hungarian army. Stephen thinks it a mere formality and is certain, as he rings the bell at the unmanned reception, that he has plenty of time to pick up the papers and head back into town for dinner with his parents.

A middle-aged woman appears begrudgingly from the back office, takes Stephen's name, and orders him to wait. Time passes as slowly as it tends to do in an empty waiting room, but Stephen is finally called in to see the sergeant.

Confidently, and with an air of impatience, Stephen tells him his story: about the unceremonious train journey and the walk to the River Don, about conditions in the camp, about the events of 13 January and his long and brutal journey back to Budapest. He includes details of the date on which he was sent out, which group he was placed in, and under which commanding officers he was stationed. The sergeant looks at Stephen blankly. He raises his eyebrows and turns his gaze down towards a piece of paper, on which he starts to scribble half-hearted notes. He looks back up at Stephen only to say: 'Wait outside, please.'

The longer Stephen waits, the more he worries. Something is beginning to feel terribly wrong. His brooding thoughts are interrupted when, finally, a soldier appears in the doorway. In a short, aggressive tone, he orders Stephen inside: 'You! Get in here . . .'

Alarmed, Stephen can't think of what to do other than to follow the soldier. He is led down a hallway and into a room. The moment he steps inside it, he immediately realises he shouldn't have, but it's too late: the soldier shuts the door and stands between it and Stephen. The room is empty and the floor is covered in straw. Stephen finds himself in a makeshift prison cell.

'We don't accept your story.' The soldier draws out the last word, forming rough air-quotations with his hands.

Perhaps because he has only just regained his strength, Stephen is unusually speechless. He has no quick-witted retort, no confident comeback. He simply did not expect to run into any such situation upon his return.

'Come on, you coward Jew, you must have escaped from your battalion.' Angry spittle sprays from the man's pasty, oval face. As his accusation is met with nothing but an incredulous stare, he softens his tone and adds in disbelief: 'No one came back from there.'

Losing patience with Stephen, who stands there dumbfounded, the soldier's voice hardens once more: 'Come on, you abandoned your post! Our men are still out there, so we're going to send you right back! Right back to Russia! Traitor!'

He clumsily stumbles out of the room and locks the door behind him. For a moment, there is silence. Stephen raises his arms and lets them drop in frustration. He hears more voices – a group of guards conversing on the other side of the door. Stephen's wits come flooding back and he addresses the disembodied voices.

'This is preposterous! On what grounds are you holding me here? Don't you dare think I don't know my rights in this country I and my father and his father's father fought for. This is not legal – I demand you let me make a phone call!'

Silence, followed by more murmurs and then, an isolated voice: 'You can make a call.'

The door swings open and Stephen is led to a telephone. He calls his safe person. On the phone with his mother, he tells her of the situation.

'It's not only that I am accused of being a defector, but they are saying that I should be sent straight back to Russia.' He tries so hard to suppress the crack in his voice as he utters the last word. At this moment, Stephen cannot think of a worse place he would care to be. Of course, he is yet to learn that there *are* worse places to be sent than Russia, and that, for him, the worst is still to come.

Katica has a plan. She assures Stephen that she is going to speak with Lorant, who has good connections within the army.

After the phone call, Stephen is ordered back into the cell-like room to wait. It's such a contrasting sight – Stephen in his finery, crouched down on the hay-covered floor. When Lorant learns of the situation, he alerts a high-ranking officer, who promptly agrees to meet with Stephen. A hammer of authority, he dismisses the soldiers' claims and advises them to discharge Stephen at once.

It wasn't a joke at all!

For the first time, I hear anger in Stephen's older voice. The wound of betrayal by his countrymen deepens.

I was threatened to be sent back. How I felt after I went through all those terrible things and all that in Russia . . . to be sent back . . . ?

The anger in his voice subsides as he falls comfortably back into a reflective tone, the audio equivalent of leaning back in an old armchair. Thinking on the bitter experience, Stephen concludes: *If I wouldn't have had this connection through my brother, I don't know what would have happened to me.*

On 3 December 1943, Stephen is walking from his bachelor apartment in Buda to Edith's shop. He thinks it right to pay her a visit, to tell her of when he last saw Laslo and to see whether she has received news of his whereabouts. A bell chimes as he pulls the shop door open. He steps inside and sees Edith behind the counter. Their eyes meet. Some moments are denser than others. A multitude of information is exchanged within a glance, in which it becomes abundantly clear that Edith has no news of Laslo Somogyi. It is upon seeing Stephen that she finally finds an outlet for her grief and, in that moment, an anger rises within her that she cannot contain.

'You?!' she shouts, her voice breaking with anger. In one swift motion, she steps out from behind the till and takes a menacing step towards Stephen, who instinctively takes a step back.

'. . . unmarried, no children, arrogant musician – you come back from this, and my husband doesn't?!' As she stands shaking in front of him, her anger turns into despair.

'It's not fair. What am I to do? I have children. I have a business to run. I am alone. Laslo isn't here, Istvan, and I have heard nothing.'

I think back on the first time Edith and Stephen met, three years prior, in that restaurant in Transylvania. Then, she was at the receiving end of Stephen's frustration. As if penned by an ill-willing poet, this meeting is just as steeped in anger, with Stephen bearing the brunt of her fury. Although it remains guesswork as to exactly why or how the feelings of animosity between them died, I know for a fact that it happened rather quickly. Shortly after this encounter, Stephen receives an invite from Edith to attend her New Year's Eve party.

My grandfather often includes dialogue in the tapes: what was said, by whom and how. Of course, I have to take into account that it is almost always exclusively through his lens of perception. Memory is a fickle and unreliable friend. In this instance, though, I can say with certainty that these words are true. Edith is with Stephen as he records his tapes. She is the silent background, the soft hiss of the tape behind his deep voice.

I didn't see that much of Mummy – we both had separate lives – she had her business to run and her children to look after. I was playing the piano.

After that 3 December meeting, Edith and Stephen go their separate ways for a short while as life, despite all of the world's turmoil, continues. Before the most jarring dissonance comes a moment of short reprieve. Seeking a sense of normality, Stephen returns to music. The Kolibri bar is a spacious and chic underground club situated in the basement of a residential apartment block, conveniently located just around the corner from his bachelor pad. War is raging and the middle and upper classes are drunk on survival. At the bar once described by a local newspaper as 'Buda's most beautiful and classy entertainment venue', they indulge in escapism, defiantly diving into raucous frenzies of jazz, drink, dance and entertainment, and Stephen provides the soundtrack. He performs almost every night. It is here that, perhaps aided by euphoria at his own survival, Stephen falls in love. Magda is a singer at the Kolibri, vivacious in character and exuding an effortless cool to rival that of his. They like each other from the moment they give their first impromptu performance together. Magda lives on her own, in an apartment even closer to the bar than Stephen's. It's there that he spends most nights of December 1943. They grow close quickly. She meets Stephen's family and gets on particularly well with Katica. Magda is not Jewish and if he'd think to look, her untroubled soul would have served as a painful warning.

New Year's Eve comes and Stephen and Lorant arrive at Edith's apartment, wine in hand. I feel a warmth when I think of that moment: my grandparents and my great-uncle celebrating, seeing out that dreadful year in style. Edith has a little upright piano in her apartment, on which her son is learning to play. When Stephen mentions my Uncle Peter in the cassette tapes – *little Peter, who was six at the time, was taking lessons* – my heart stops and, much as it had done when I first heard Stephen mention my seven-year-old dad, time stands still.

Edith asks Stephen to play piano and, of course, he obliges. Throwing themselves into a joyous medley of their favourite songs, they sing and dance together, greeting the new and fateful year with the most powerful force us humans can call upon: unity in song, happiness and hope. It is all the sweeter in the knowledge of just how fleeting a reprieve it is.

We had a nice time, although the darker, darker clouds were already on the horizon.

No matter how many times I listen to Stephen's composition 'The Old Mill', I always find myself swept up in its drama. After a slow and steady build, the frenetic energy reaches its peak when the right-hand melody whirls around in wild little circles and is interspersed with a polyphony of syncopated countermelodies and sharp, dissonant chords.

The unfolding of events over the next three months reminds me of this. Its build-up, too, is a slow and deceitful crescendo until March 1944, when everything seems to happen at once.

Stephen is still performing most nights at the Kolibri and spends all his spare time exploiting the freedom he still possesses, in togetherness with Magda and his family. On the global stage, Hitler is fearing the loss of yet another ally. Italy had changed allegiance just as Stephen was recuperating in Budapest's military hospital. Fighting alongside Hitler, Hungary has by now lost tens of thousands of soldiers and the Horthy/Kallay government is starting to reconsider. It is important to note that the change of heart has little to do with any kind of moral backbone. (Minister Kallay, while he was at this point still protecting Hungarian Jews from the worst, calls for a 'radical solution' to the 'Jewish problem' after the war.) Rather it is brought upon by the cold realisation that they find themselves on the losing side of the war. In an attempt to emulate Italy, the government allows partial relaxation of Third-Reich-imposed censorship, which in turn swiftly results in demands from the opposition for Hungary's withdrawal from the war. Foolishly, Hungary's government ignore intelligence stating that a German invasion is imminent. Kallay is more concerned by the approaching Russian army and a potential Bolshevik threat to the status quo and doesn't heed the Allies' call to defend Hungary's borders against a possible German occupation. While most Hungarian Jews – Stephen included – were making the fatal error of believing, even now, after the stripping away of rights, that their country would not sell them out, Hungary's government felt a similar false sense of security. It did not countenance the idea that Germany would overrun them by force.

On 12 March, Adolf Hitler states: 'For some time it has been known to me and the Reich government that the Hungarian Kallay government has prepared Hungary's betrayal of the European Nations. The Jews, who control everything in Hungary, and individual reactionary or partly Jewish and corrupt elements of the Hungarian aristocracy, have brought the Hungarian people, who were well disposed towards us, in this situation.'

On 19 March, German troops invade and occupy Hungary. It comes as no surprise that the blame for the suffering Hitler's invasion brings upon the country and its people is placed upon vulnerable, persecuted shoulders. While Miklos Horthy is permitted to stay in his position of power, Minister Kallay is replaced by a pro-German fanatical, General Dome Sztojay. Under his rule, the far-right ultranationalist party known as the Arrow Cross bring on a regime of cruel and arbitrary terror against the Jews of Budapest. Accompanying them is Adolf Eichmann – orchestrator of the Holocaust. Heading up a special unit, it is his job to oversee the implementation of the 'final solution', the deportation and systematic mass murder of Hungary's Jews.

Within days of the invasion, a flurry of additional anti-Jewish decrees are passed. Jewish-run businesses are confiscated. Jewish-owned bank accounts are closed, the money seized. Jews are no longer permitted phones or radios. Jews have to declare all their valuables and are often forced to give them up, including wedding bands, cigarette cases – anything of monetary value. Jews are forced to wear the yellow Star of David on their clothing, visible at all times, making them an open target to abuse and violence in public. Across the country, Jewish families are forced out of their homes and into urban ghettos, in which several families are crammed into one apartment. Sometimes, the ghettos encompass the area of a former Jewish neighbourhood; other times, it is a single building: a residential apartment block, a factory or a school. In some Hungarian cities, Jews are even forced to live outdoors, without any kind of shelter or sanitary facilities. Throughout, food and water supplies are dangerously inadequate. The ghettos are guarded by the gendarmerie and individual police officers often torture those trapped inside and extort valuables from them for their personal gain. Instruments often slip through the net and remain permitted. Trust the ill-intentioned to underestimate the power of music.

Within weeks, my family, like thousands of those suffering similar fates, are stripped of their human rights and torn out of society's fabric – the very fabric they had helped weave over the past two hundred years. Aladar and Katica are forced to take meticulous stock of all their inventory, which takes days. Every last item pertaining to their business, along with documents and keys to any real estate, have to be handed over to the authorities. Poor Edith, alone with her two little children, is forced to do the same, as are Aladar's brothers, bringing the empire of S. Holtzer & Sons to a temporary halt.

During these first weeks of the occupation, hundreds of Jews – both men and women – are violently beaten, harassed, isolated and murdered by the Arrow Cross gangs. Across Hungary, families like mine are scrambling to mobilise and to hide and keep safe as many of their possessions as they can. Tormented by frequent and random visits by Nazi officials, during which they sometimes legally and sometimes illegally confiscate whatever they please, Katica decides to entrust Magda with some of her most treasured belongings for safe-keeping, such as jewellery, clothing and a couple of Persian rugs. Let me share, as a moment of light relief, that among the possessions bestowed upon Stephen's much-liked girlfriend are his vast collection of dress shirts. On the tapes, Stephen recalls giving her seventy of his silk shirts, which he apparently 'needed for performing'.

'Did you need seventy silk shirts?' I laugh and ask out loud, momentarily forgetting once again that Stephen isn't in the room with me.

Stephen's relationship with Magda, of course, had become illegal from one day to the next, as Jews are now prohibited from fraternising with non-Jewish people. At first, though, they continue to see one another defiantly.

When I was a child, my dad told me about how some of our family members had to take in strangers to their homes because it became illegal to have spare rooms. I don't remember grasping the historical context of this, but I do remember vividly the injustice I felt upon learning this fact. To my childlike mind, this was the height of indignity and a horrific thought – complete strangers appearing in your kitchen, using your bathroom, possibly even playing with your toys. Of course, the image I held in my mind did not match the much darker reality, in which sometimes up to twenty starving and desperate people were forced to live together in one room, having to sleep on chairs and floors. There are strict curfews, and even stricter ones for Jewish women, allowing them to leave their cramped quarters for only a couple of hours a day.

While some of my relatives are forced to open their homes, others have to abandon theirs. Aladar and Katica's apartment in St Stephen's Square is too desirable an address to be turned into a Jewish ghetto. Instead, they are relocated to one of the many designated 'yellow-star buildings'. They are forced to leave behind their home with most everything in it – the furniture, the family paintings and the Blüthner baby grand piano. They hope that this is temporary, that they will be able to return to it soon, but uncertainty weighs heavy on their hearts.

Our piano is not a sentient being – I know this – but I believe it has memory. A part of Stephen never left that apartment. Songwriting is a mysterious craft that, at its best, is no craft at all. The finest ideas present themselves, pristine and fully formed, to the artist, finding just the right moment to pass like an electric current through their being, filtering through their experience and finally spilling out of their fingertips and onto the ivory keys. The exchange of energy is as real as it is magical. As heart-wrenching as it must have been to leave it behind, the piano keeps an imprint of its players within it. It stands there, full of its players' emotions, wishing its earthly bodies well on their journey. It sings a quiet song of memory and will patiently await their return.

Fighting its way through the dissonant eruptions of inhumanity echoing through Hungary's capital is a song of resistance. Many individuals take it upon themselves to save the lives of the persecuted and are speaking up for the voiceless. Several Swiss and Swedish diplomats start to issue protective passports to Jewish Hungarians in a bid to save them. One of the most prominent is Swedish architect and businessman Raoul Wallenberg who, serving as Sweden's special envoy in Budapest, manages to issue hundreds of protective passports and starts setting up safe houses for Hungarian Jews in buildings he declares as Swedish territory.

His Swiss counterpart Carl Lutz sets up a total of seventy-six safe houses across Budapest. The most famous, the Glass House (an old glass factory), is situated just around the corner from Aladar and Katica's apartment in St Stephen's Square. Apart from sheltering up to three thousand Hungarian Jews, it also functions as the headquarters for the Jewish youth underground movement.

When the Nazi government starts deporting Hungarian Jews to the death camps, Carl Lutz swiftly negotiates a special deal, gaining permission to issue protective letters to eight thousand Hungarian Jews. Lutz deliberately misinterprets his remit – issuing papers to eight thousand families rather than eight thousand individuals, saving tens of thousands of additional lives.

I have managed to get such a Swiss certificate, which was of course issued with my photograph on it.

Stephen manages to procure a letter of protection issued by the Red Cross. Lorant gets papers and George, a temporary document holding the promise that safe papers are on the way. While it is a little unclear why some members of the family were able to procure safe papers and others weren't, it seems to have been something of a lottery. Having such papers also wasn't a sure protection. For Stephen, while they should be enough to protect him from the worst, they don't save him from having to move into his own 'yellow star' accommodation. In early April, he is forced to move out of his apartment and ordered to assemble at a nearby school. Without phones or radios, it's now much harder for Jewish citizens to stay in touch with family and loved ones. The weaponised isolation results in a breakdown of networks to pass on any information, personal or political. The very passing on of news becomes extremely risky, a political act with potentially dire consequences.

Stephen, therefore, has little contact with his family; not knowing their fate adds to his distress. It makes one incident that Stephen shares in the tapes all the more remarkable. One evening at the school, he hears his name. The voice is familiar, but due to the unexpected nature of the visit, it takes Stephen a while to place it. With a furrowed brow, he listens to the voice as it grows louder in the hallway, asking repeatedly: 'Excuse me, do you know an Istvan Bastyai?'

It is met with a mumbling of strangers, saying they do not. When Stephen finally recognises the voice, he jumps to his feet and jogs towards it. As he twists his body through the doorframe to peer down the corridor, he sees him: the caretaker of Aladar and Katica's home. After a brief moment of joy as the men greet one another with a handshake and an embrace, Stephen realises the man's face is pale and glinting with beads of sweat. His expression is one of worry.

'What is it?' Stephen asks, wide-eyed.

'There are rumours . . .' the man says anxiously, his eyes darting around nervously as he inches closer to Stephen before continuing.

'The yellow-star building where your parents are – there are rumours that everyone in that building is being deported tomorrow.'

A swarm of feelings rush through Stephen's being: gratitude towards the informant, anger at the inhumanity at play, and helplessness as he thinks what, if anything, he can possibly do to prevent his greatest fear from becoming reality. In that moment, an idea crystallises in his mind, pristine and clear as they often do in times of crisis.

'Can you wait here?' he asks the caretaker hastily, one hand placed urgently on his shoulder.

The caretaker cranes his neck around as if to see whether anyone would stop him from doing so, before replying: 'Yes, of course.' And with that, Stephen turns around and ducks back into the room he shares with countless others.

He kneels on the floor before his bunk, turning his back to the room so as to conceal his actions. From the inside of his jacket, he pulls out a folded document – his Swiss papers. Carefully, he unfolds it and places it on the bed before him. From the inside of his sock, he retrieves a leather wallet, from which he pulls the only photograph he carries with him.

'Here.' Stephen's back in the hallway and holds out the document to the caretaker, who swiftly takes it and puts it in his coat pocket.

'Can you take this to them, please? Now? It should hopefully keep them safe,' he says, before adding, 'And this. Can you take this for them as well, please?'

He reaches around his neck and hands over his mother's necklace, the little golden four-leafed clover shimmering in the otherwise dreary hallway. The caretaker promises to go to them without delay and wishes Stephen well.

I wasn't caring much about myself or my safety, but of course I was very concerned with my parents' safety. Now what I did was I took my photograph out and replaced it with the photographs of my father and mother so that this certificate would protect them instead of me.

This, I did not know. As I sit listening to Stephen's story for the first time, I am overcome with emotion at this revelation and have to pause his retelling to allow the tears to come. I have the cruelty of hindsight and know, at least in broad terms, what this sacrifice will mean for Stephen. There is no way of knowing to what extent he understood in this moment what the ramifications of forging his papers to be in his parents' names would be, but I am certain Stephen didn't consider any other option for even a second. Their fur coat had saved him; his Swiss papers might save them in return.

A peculiar thing is happening: the distance between my grandfather and me is shrinking. The emotions I'm experiencing are so intense and my reactions so visceral, they do not feel entirely my own. I let them guide me as I follow Stephen, filling in the blanks in his retelling with intuition, a generational knowing.

And yet, there is still a part of me that on occasion questions just how reliable a narrator Stephen is. It is perhaps natural to feel a sense of incredulity at one person's story being so full of fantastical chance, coincidences, narrow misses and heroism. But the more stories I read, particularly those written by second- and third-generation survivors of the Holocaust such as myself, the more I see that I am not alone with this. It is a self-preservation mechanism, as though my subconscious is working hard to stop myself from engaging too much with the hurt of the past. It is easier to think that Stephen exaggerated some of the horrific details, that he didn't see people die because they pulled their trousers down in the snow. It's easier to think that he wasn't faced with the drastic choice of saving himself or his parents. It is easier to doubt than it is to accept and feel the breadth of emotions, including my own survival guilt, as a consequence. Truthfully, a sense of self-importance and even selfishness are traits that many surviving members of my family would assign to Stephen. And so I find myself wondering, if only briefly, whether this may have been a self-aggrandising moment in his retelling – a story he may have exaggerated over time – or whether it is true that he sacrificed himself to save his parents. It is, of course, easy to say that I would have done the same, but unlike Stephen, I do not have the arrogance to think I know for certain how I would handle a situation so far outside of my own comprehension.

Months after I first listened to this part of Stephen's story, I visit the Wiener Holocaust Library in London. I'm here to research and to write, as well as to look through some of Stephen's photo albums which are stored here. A couple of years prior, I had accompanied Julie as she deposited the albums to the library for safekeeping. As I climb the stairs and enter the beautiful reading room, I am greeted by the friendly staff, who have already retrieved Stephen's photo albums from the impressive basement archives. It is the first time I have looked through these photographs since I started on my journey with Stephen. I carefully turn the pages and there, I see it. Unassumingly positioned between photos of Stephen's youth, his performances and his friends and girlfriends, is a photograph – a landscape shot of five people walking down a wide street towards the photographer. The second and fourth person have been cut out, leaving rectangular holes throughout the length of the photograph. Upon closer inspection, I can see the man on the far right of the photo is Lorant dressed in his soldier's uniform. The pretty girl in a three-quarter-length dress on the far left is Annie. The stately-looking man in the middle is József, Annie's husband. To the right of this strange, cut-out photo is a fragment of a document, upon which a photo of Katica, so clearly cut out and taken from that group shot, is glued. The photo and fragment of paper around it is stamped with what looks like the Swiss flag. In the margins of this photo album page, I read in Stephen's handwriting: 'Mother & Father's pictures – saved them from deportation.'

Within the next two months, nearly 440,000 Hungarian Jews are deported in more than 145 trains. Many of them are headed to Auschwitz, the most notorious of the extermination camps. Roughly eight thousand, though, are selected for forced labour. My grandfather is one of them.

At the end of April, Stephen and the other occupants of the school are rounded up and put in a cattle wagon. Without any safeguarding papers, there is nothing in his power to convince the authorities otherwise. The train travels west, taking him to a large ghetto at Hungary's Austrian border called Sopron. Stephen once again finds himself in good company. Among his fellow prisoners are several acquaintances, as well as his Cousin Bela, the son of his Uncle Emil. The conditions at Sopron are harsh. Upon arrival, the inmates are given wooden shoes and ordered to wear them as well as the yellow Star of David at all times. The shoes serve the cruel purpose of alerting guards to their movements – wearing them, it is impossible to move without being heard. They sleep in barracks and work all day digging defensive trenches for the German army, preparing for the inevitable arrival of Russian tanks.

The ghetto of Sopron is not heavily guarded. A little 'gypsy boy', as Stephen describes him, dives in and out of it undetected, offering to procure small pleasures – cigarettes and alcohol – for the inmates in exchange for a bit of money. With his small and unassuming frame, he manages to dodge in and out of Sopron without any of the guards noticing or caring. Inspired by his gall, Stephen decides to take a risk.

I was very daring – because I wanted to see the woman I loved.

A strong song of defiance still sings out in Stephen's heart as he rips the yellow star from his sleeve and shoves it into his trouser pocket one morning. He silently slides out of his wooden shoes and into his streetwear. Then, with purpose, Stephen walks out of Sopron and catches a train back to Budapest to meet with Magda in her apartment. He is aware of the risk he is taking – if he is caught, the likely outcome will be death by the Arrow Cross army.

Stephen's hubris permeates this story – the little boy playing dead on the ground sabotaging child's play; the young man throwing his hands up to the sky, telling his mother that 'my hands are my money' as an affirmation of his self-belief in his piano playing; the defiant prisoner with an iron determination to survive. As I picture him, stealing back his freedom, I think on how the risks we take and the decisions we make become our story. A certain recklessness echoes through my family and I wonder if those waves were caused by him. Among us, there is certainly a disposition towards following our own path, in defiance of norms and expectations. The risk-taking, at its best, manifests in bold life choices underpinned by a strong sense of self-belief, but it rears its head in uglier ways, too. We are not great at taking care of ourselves or keeping safe. Our priorities lie elsewhere, with work, or the wellbeing of others. We share a tendency to push ourselves to and often beyond our limits. Something within makes us feel a need to justify our very existence, indebted to all the suffering that came before it.

Stephen escapes the Sopron ghetto on several occasions to spend time with Magda and to exploit every possible moment of freedom. He is well aware that he is risking his life each time he rips the yellow Star of David off his jacket, stuffs it into his pocket and slips out of the ghetto to catch a train to Budapest. He often contemplates trying to find his parents, but this would involve visiting Jewish safe houses, which, on reflection, he deems too risky. He is happy to risk his own life, but he cannot bear the thought of endangering his family. If he were caught, he'd undoubtedly be killed. If he were caught with his parents or siblings, it is likely that their lives would also be on the line. His non-Jewish girlfriend seems a safer partner in crime for his defiant acts of rebellion.

I believe my grandfather may have never truly loved Magda. Given the timescale, it seems likely that their relationship was of a moment, swept up in a frenzy of circumstance. Intense realities make excellent breeding grounds for intense fantasy. Stephen may also have felt a strong desire to not repeat the mistakes he had made with Roszi, directing all his efforts towards not failing at another relationship. For whatever reason, a distance grows between Stephen and Magda despite, or perhaps even because of, the high-risk nature of their affair. For a while now, he has felt her pull away and one day he arrives at her apartment door at the arranged time, but Magda doesn't answer. Stephen daren't knock too loudly or call out her name for fear of being noticed by a neighbour – a swift call from any one of them would result in his arrest and, most likely, his death. Instead, he turns the door handle and pushes lightly against the front door with his shoulder. To his surprise, it's unlocked and opens with ease. Adrenalin rushes through Stephen's body as he closes the door behind him and moves the latch across the inside lock. Slowly, he walks through the apartment. He finds himself quite alone, with no sign of Magda. No sooner has he allowed himself to exhale, he jumps in fright as there's a loud and angry knock on the front door.

'Police!'

Stephen freezes, his wide-eyed gaze turned towards the door and the voice behind it. Another harsh rap of knuckles breaks the silence and sends a current of panic down Stephen's spine.

'Hello? Is anybody home? Open the door!'

Stephen's eyes widen even further, taken aback by the violence in the voice of the invisible man behind the door. As he meets it with icy silence, he hears a murmur, as if one man is holding back and talking down another.

A second voice, lower in volume and aggression, tries to elicit a response: 'Police – open the door!'

With the sound of diminishing footsteps Stephen's mind fills with a flurry of thoughts. The most pressing question is why Magda isn't here to meet him. He knows in this moment that their relationship is over and that he most likely will not see Magda Gutfreund again. The more painful and lingering question is whether she simply grew too afraid and didn't have the strength to tell him to his face, or whether this was a deadly and deliberate deceit. Stephen would never be sure if Magda had denounced him to the authorities or not.

Back at Sopron, he learns that she is seeing someone else. I have no way of knowing her side of this story and have no desire to second guess her intentions, but I do know that no one in my family ever saw Magda again. She disappears from this story, along with Katica's jewellery and Stephen's seventy silk dress shirts, leaving him with a sense that he has overdone his taking of risks. Fatefully, this would be the last time Stephen breaks the rules.

At Sopron, conditions worsen. Stephen remembers two incidents in which the Nazi commanders torment and kill, simply to demonstrate their power. One day, Stephen and the other prisoners are ordered to line up by the trenches they are digging, their wooden shoes caked in mud. The Nazi commander walks down the line, arbitrarily stops and shoots every tenth man, their bodies falling into the freshly dug trenches.

On another occasion, a guard fires shots at random into the crowds. One of the bullets narrowly misses the top of Stephen's head. He feels the force of it as he stands there, rooted to the ground in shock. The shooter had deliberately missed, wanting simply to torture the vulnerable people suffering under his reign.

You can imagine our fright and terror to go through an incident like that.

That night, Stephen lies awake and stares at the bunk above him. He's so lost in thought that he hardly notices his Cousin Bela slip into the barrack. Stephen turns his head, resting listlessly on his folded arms, to meet his cousin's gaze. Before him is a curious sight – Bela stands, dressed in a smart overcoat, a hat and dress shoes, his confident figure comically out of place, clashing with the defeated faces failing to fall asleep around them. Bela turns to Stephen: 'Aren't you coming?'

'Aren't I coming where?' he asks wryly.

'I've had enough. I'm leaving!' Bela's words are as simple as though he was bidding his early farewell at a dinner party. Stephen sits up, not breaking his questioning stare.

'I'm going to escape, back to Budapest and go into hiding,' Bela states matter-of-factly. 'Aren't you coming with me?'

We are the decisions we make and the risks we take. In this moment, Stephen does not have it in him to find the loophole. The blow of the gun and Magda's recent rejection dull his tone and a cloud of all the dark realities settles in – the deep fear for his family; a hatred for the brutal, forced detachment from them and the hopelessness of his own situation. Stephen decides that this is a risk he cannot take.

'I can't go,' he says slowly, as if searching in his mind for options while he's speaking. 'I haven't got anywhere *to* go! What are you going to do? Where are you going?' he asks, a mild annoyance now rising within him.

'I have a girlfriend who will hide me away – I'll stay with her.'

I don't have anyone, says the voice in Stephen's mind as a loneliness engulfs him. He doesn't utter the words out loud, but simply nods, mustering a half-smile before getting up to say goodbye to his cousin.

Bela took a risk that day. With his head held high and dressed in his finery, he walked out of Sopron. He followed through with his plan, successfully hiding in Budapest before seeking refuge and settling in South America.

I grew up in a newly reunified Germany. At school, I studied the rise of Hitler and the unimaginable atrocities of the Holocaust in various stages of my education. I remember one of my classmates raising their hand in political science class in 12th Grade (the British equivalent to sixth form) when my teacher announced what the focus of the first semester would be: 'But we already studied this in Year Ten. How come we're covering the Holocaust again?'

'So that it never happens again.'

My teacher's reply was so sharp and immediate, it's stayed with me. He continued, his words now much calmer and deliberately slow: 'Here in Germany we have a responsibility. You need to learn every detail about how Hitler came to power legally so that you can ensure that something like this never happens again in your lifetime.'

In Year Eight (at the age of fourteen), I got my parents to write me a note, excusing me from the otherwise compulsory school trip to a concentration camp. I couldn't put it into words at the time, but I had a strong feeling that my grandparents, who at this point were no longer with us, didn't want me to go anywhere near a camp. The trauma they held in their bones echoed in mine.

I put off listening to the next part of Stephen's story for a long time.

CHAPTER 16

So That It Never Happens Again

But coming back to the serious . . . the serious happenings.

Soon after Bela leaves, Sopron is evacuated. One morning in either late May or early June, Stephen and the other inmates are ordered to assemble and to start marching. The Nazi officials march them to the Austrian border. Here, they are joined by several other groups of Jewish men, women and children from all corners of Hungary. One of five thousand, Stephen is paraded through the Austrian district of Burgenland, through villages, towns and the countryside, towards their next destination. History will refer to these walks as death marches, a befitting and chilling description of my grandfather's experiences. They are marched through villages, former neighbours and friends witnessing the atrocities.

They are herded along roads, uniformed soldiers to either side of them, some bearing rifles, others brandishing truncheons. As they start to arbitrarily beat the prisoners, panic breaks out. Terrified, they make a run for it in their clunky, wooden shoes. Many, already exhausted from months of mistreatment and malnourishment in labour camps and ghettos, simply collapse on the way and die. The death march goes on throughout the day.

As you can imagine, a lot of people running . . . some of them fell, and some of them were pushed over. Everyone who fell was shot.

The sun sets, the path before them bathed in a cold, silver light. The Nazi officials force them off the road and into a field, driving them like cattle, and order them to line up. Stephen remembers vividly the feel of the rough, dry earth beneath his feet and that it was a full moon.

'Well, this is it,' Stephen mutters under his breath, looking to his left and right in an attempt to make eye contact with the people he thinks he's about to die next to, convinced they are all going to be murdered.

But that wasn't the case, it was just a way to frighten and terrorise the poor defenceless people.

They are forced to stand in the field, shivering from the cold, until the sun rises. Then, the death march continues until they finally reach a train station somewhere south of Vienna. Those who have made it this far are shoved into cattle wagons again. In the train, there's no room to move. They stand there for hours, shoulder to shoulder in the darkness, before the wagon finally sets off. In that time and for the duration of the journey they are not given any food or water. There are no sanitary breaks.

The train has been standing for hours and hours; the guards came and people who died from hunger were just thrown out of the trains and that was that.

They arrive at the concentration camp Mauthausen at night. When Stephen is finally let out of the train, he is so hungry that he desperately pulls up tufts of grass from the ground and eats it. *Like cattle*, he jokes in his retelling, and a chill runs down my spine.

The leaves clung on to their branches for an unusual amount of time the year my dad died, so that when we held his funeral – and it still feels strange calling it that as it was such a joyous celebration of his life

– the foliage was still boasting a beautiful bright red and orange in deepest November. Finally, the leaves withered and dropped, bringing a winter upon my world. A part of me was offended when they dared reappear the following spring. I felt affronted by their delicate pinks and light greens. Then, I looked upon them as a curious bystander, oddly detached from the cycle of nature and the passing of time, before finally accepting them as the first signs of a first spring without him. Nature shows little regard for our emotions and cares not about the various plots and subplots of our lives. As cruel as its disregard for our own existence can feel, it is actually a comfort. Seasons continue to change in an infinite cycle of dying and rebirth, even throughout the darkest moments of our collective time on earth.

Stephen does not speak much of his time in the concentration camp. His voice an emotionless monotone, he sums up the following year in minutes in the tapes, choosing to highlight only a few details, none of which adequately portray what historical document-ation unfortunately proves he must have experienced. The notes we choose to omit are just as important as the ones we play.

So far, Stephen has taken me by the hand and guided me through his life – a front-row seat to his childhood, music career, love life, hardships and survival – but he does not take me here. As I realise this, I find myself overcome with sorrow, mourning his aloneness. Like so many others who lived through such deeply traumatic times, Stephen never spoke about the horrors.

Mauthausen was one of the most brutal and severe of the Nazi concentration camps. The inmates suffered not only from malnutri-tion, overcrowded huts and constant abuse and beatings by the guards and kapos, but also from exceptionally hard labour.

I am on the Mauthausen Memorial website. It's a peculiar sensation reading up on the details. There is a part of me that feels Stephen doesn't want me to know. It feels rude, an intrusion of his privacy, to read about the cruel history of the concentration camp. And it feels so real. His reluctance pulsing through me, I experience a chill followed by a wave of exhaustion when I try to focus on this chapter of the story. It is an impossible task, to speak of the unspeakable. I keep going back and forth, failing to settle on whether I should honour Stephen's silence and share nothing more than what he has committed to tape, or whether his story needs underpinning with the horrible truths of history. I realise that a part of me is still afraid to tie my family to this darkness. I hope that Stephen forgives me if I share some of the background to the camp and the horrors that happened around him. My intention, seeing as I cannot undo the past, is to use Stephen's story to help prevent it from becoming our future.

New prisoners arrive at Mauthausen every day. It is a large operation with a complex hierarchical structure, its spidery arms executing the will of a far-removed head. 'I was just following orders,' is an ugly sentence lodged still in the German psyche. At first, Mauthausen holds mostly political opponents, questioners of the Nazi regime and Soviet prisoners of war. Soon, though, Jews from across Europe are deported to the camp. In May 1944, the first group of roughly eight thousand Hungarian Jews arrives from Auschwitz. I can't find any records of a death march from Sopron to Mauthausen, but it is likely that Stephen arrives at the camp around this time.

Upon arrival, prisoners are lined up and assessed. They are divided into two groups, each sent to different shower chambers. One group, deemed fit to work, are stripped naked, showered and shaved, removing every last strand of body hair. Stripped of any belongings that may tie an individual to their former life – clothing, glasses, hair – they are given prison uniforms, assigned a number and put to work – a new and naked existence. The other group, deemed useless, are murdered in the gas chambers.

Stephen does share that upon arrival, Mauthausen is already full. There is no room in the barracks – instead, he sleeps in a tent, in which hundreds of prisoners seek refuge each night, lying side by side on the cold, frozen mud. Most prisoners are forced to sleep outside, huddled together for warmth underneath scraps of blanket. In the tents, he sees many familiar, yet emaciated, faces. It is the grimmest of reunions.

I met many of my very old friends, back from my school days and even from afterwards in Budapest.

The Holocaust was a serious money maker, the exploitation of forced labourers highly lucrative. Prisoners aided German war efforts, were rented out to nearby farms and factories, were experimented on by medical corporations and rinsed for any and all of their resources, including money, possessions, down to a person's last leather belt and boots, to the gold in their teeth, their flesh and bone. The Mauthausen Memorial website states that 'its production output was unparalleled'.

The camp was built around a quarry, in which thousands of prisoners are forced to work gruelling eleven-hour shifts in the most brutal of conditions. Set in the mountains, the camp reached extreme temperatures, resulting in countless deaths when prisoners would collapse in the heat or freeze to death. Initially, prisoners who could no longer work were transported to a nearby crematorium, to be exterminated there. Over time, this became too expensive and

Mauthausen built its own gas chambers and crematorium on site to kill and dispose of the dead.

Some of the details of forced labour at Mauthausen read as though they are taken out of the darker parts of Greek mythology, rather than torture methods employed within the last century. I read about the 'stairs of death': 182 steps that led from the base of the quarry up to the top of the cliff, the so-called 'Parachutists' Wall'.

The prisoners, carrying heavy blocks of stone, are made to run up the stairs one behind the other. Many collapse and fall to their death, taking those behind with them. Those who survive are lined up on the cliff's edge and are forced, at gun-point, to make a decision between being shot or pushing the man next in line off the cliff.

One of the few things that Stephen shares is how little food they are given. Each day, he says, they are served 'some sort of soup'. By cruel design, the amount they are presented with is not nearly enough for all inmates to eat. The prisoners are made to fight one another for the last drops of it.

'Who knows what he did to survive?' Julie says in a monotone not unlike that of Stephen's on the tape, as she stares into the distance while we are discussing this part of his story.

Stephen doesn't mention what he is forced to do or experience in the camp. He is able, somehow, to endure the work. The average life expectancy of a prisoner at Mauthausen is six months. Stephen is here for just under a year. In this time, he discovers he has a macabre skill: *I acquired a very wide knowledge of looking at people's faces and knowing in advance that this person is not going to make it – even if he was maybe days or weeks away from his end.* Stephen describes looking into his friends' eyes and knowing whether or not they would survive.

There is a photograph in Stephen's album of a young man I do not recognise. It looks like it could be an official school portrait. The boy is wearing a suit and tie. He has light skin and dark hair and is wearing those thick, round spectacles so common in Jewish communities. At first glance, I thought it might be a photograph of a younger Stephen. But while this boy too has delicate, handsome facial features, he really doesn't look much like my grandfather at all. The picture below – one of a shirtless Stephen wearing his boxing gloves and a steely stare – highlights their differences. Thumbing through Stephen's photo albums, I've often wondered about this photo. Stephen is usually rather descriptive in the margins, but this page, containing the two photos, is simply titled: 'Me as I was then', which had at first led me to believe that the photo of the boy was that of Stephen, caught at an odd stage of puberty. Nobody seems to know who he is and I wonder why Stephen held on to the picture. As I'm writing these chapters and looking through the album once more, I carefully remove the protective plastic and lift the picture up from the page. I turn it over and see Stephen's handwriting: 'A grammar school friend of mine from Szeged – died in MAUTHAUSEN concentration camp after I have seen him there – his name was Leslie PARTOS.'

And now I understand why Stephen kept the photo, placing it with one from his youth. One boy will go on to fill many pages of photo albums, the other will not be so lucky. Leslie, a 'me' that Stephen so easily could have been.

Due to the overcrowding and terrible conditions, as well as deliberate infection caused by injections administered by the sadistic medical professionals working in the camps, many diseases spread through the prisoner population. Typhoid fever is one such – it rips through the camp and many die from it, but Stephen doesn't.

Unbeknownst to him at the time, having already recovered from typhoid fever after his walk back from forced labour in Russia, he is immune.

At some point, word among the prisoners spreads that the ovens, used to cremate the bodies of the thousands of men, women and children who are murdered in the gas chambers, are broken. For hundreds of tired and ill inmates, this will mean their life is prolonged by the luck of the draw.

I can't find any documentation to validate Stephen's stay at Mauthausen. The Wiener Library holds evidence of his imprisonment at Sopron, but without a prison number issued at the concentration camp, they cannot find him in Mauthausen's records. I learn that due to overcrowding, many prisoners – particularly those who stayed in tents – were never properly registered. To add to the chaos, prisoners arriving at the camps were often allocated numbers of those who had already been killed. Furthermore, much of the camp's files and evidence was deliberately destroyed.

I do find eyewitness accounts and references to Stephen's next part of his story. In April 1945, Mauthausen is bursting at its seams, littered with emaciated, corpse-like figures. Meanwhile, the Russian army is approaching. On 14 April, the commander of Mauthausen decides to evacuate the camp.

Two days after the decision is made, Stephen is placed in the first of three groups and is put on yet another death march. They walk south of Mauthausen until they hit the nearby town of Ents. From there, they head west, walking for a torturous four days until they reach the forests around Mauthausen's newest sub camp, Gunskirchen.

In a bid to avoid starvation, Stephen grasps what he can while he walks, shoving tufts of grass, leaves and nettles into his mouth. Many around him collapse. Anyone who falls behind or out of step is shot. Stephen witnesses Nazi officials murder countless prisoners on the way to Gunskirchen. Some of the dead are crudely buried; others are left on the roadside, leaving behind them a macabre trail.

The eyewitness accounts of those less reluctant to share the horrific details give me a darker insight into what Stephen will have experienced along the way. An unnamed man says how on one occasion, fifty men were sent ahead to dig graves for the dead. A Nazi soldier disapproved of one of the gravediggers' work and ordered him to stand in the grave. There, he beat him to death. The eyewitness shares that 'one could see the inner parts of his skull, that is how much he beat him. It was a terrible view. The others then covered him with soil.'

Death marches such as this one were witnessed by many. The tortured prisoners were often led through populated spaces, such as villages and towns. Photographic evidence from the time shows onlookers standing idly by, gathered at the side of the street or watching from the safety of their own homes. Some even chose to participate, hurling abuse and objects from open windows.

Of all the horrors he recounts, it is this – the public's complicity – that evokes audible emotion in Stephen's retelling. There's a quiver in his voice, making him sound for the first time despondent, as he reflects:

The population was absolutely cold and immune to any such a scene and some of them must have seen us because we went through villages as well.

Gunskirchen is a small camp situated in a clearing in the middle of a deep forest. It consists of eleven barracks, one of which serves as accommodation for the Nazi officers. Built to hold about four thousand prisoners, it is estimated that by the time Stephen arrives, over three times that number are fighting for survival in the most dire of conditions.

As Stephen arrives, the camp is coated in mud and already littered with death. He slips and slides in the filth as he makes his way to one of the barracks. There is an eerie calm among the prisoners, all energy spent on clinging to life – a slow and resigned pulse. Among the commanders, Stephen feels a frenetic energy as they dart across the camp, Alsatian and Dobermann dogs at their booted heels, baring jagged teeth, trained to rip people apart on command. The guards are more erratic, shooting people for the most minor infringements: for looking the wrong way, for standing too straight.

There is no forced labour at Gunskirchen. There is also hardly any food, water or sanitation. It looks to Stephen as though this is the place they have been sent to die. Occasionally, they are served turnip soup, but not on a daily basis. There are two rusty taps in the camp – when Stephen gets a hold of a modest amount of water, he can't decide whether to drink it or use it to wash. There are no facilities; to 'do their necessary business', prisoners squat in the open over trenches.

Stephen isn't telling this story in his mother tongue of Hungarian. I notice that his immigrant English is often peppered with the occasional German word. Describing this detail, he uses the German word for 'squatting' and upon first listening, I don't even notice it. To me, a seamless weaving in and out of English and German is my mother tongue. It is a sweet moment of comfort in a very bitter symphony to learn that this is something we have in common.

People had to do their necessary things by 'hocking' down. Whether you were a female or male, it didn't make any difference whatsoever . . .

Stephen loses track of how many days pass at Gunskirchen, but he guesses it to be the month of May by now. Rumour spreads that the Americans are coming. His last days at the camp are most likely spent disposing of the many dead bodies strewn across the camp. The stronger prisoners are ordered to dig a mass grave and throw the bodies into it.

One morning, he awakes to an eerie silence. He is used to the quiet of the weak and the dying within the barracks, but the absence of German voices outside in the camp is disorientating. With great effort, Stephen climbs over bodies and out of the wooden hut. The scene before him is one of surreal serenity. The Germans are gone. Stephen doesn't know it at the time, but the last of the guards had left before sunrise, escaping the camp and into the night in civilian clothes. There is no movement, save for the Alsatian dogs, now wandering aimlessly and ownerless around the camp. Stephen takes one frail and tentative step further out into the grounds. Those who still have the strength to walk are soon to follow him out of the barracks. They huddle there in confused silence, which is suddenly interrupted by a rumbling noise. In the distance, they see jeeps and American flags.

'Does anybody speak English?' Captain J. D. Pletcher calls out.

Several men point at Stephen.

'He does!'

Stephen looks around in surprise. He knows he's not the only one who can communicate in English, but before he can form a response, an American soldier stretches out his hand.

'What's your name, sir?'

It is jarring to Stephen to be met with respect, the outstretched hand taking him by surprise. When he opens his mouth to speak, his voice comes out rough, as if he hasn't used it in years.

'Stephen,' he says, giving the English version of his name, and in that moment, a sense of self comes flooding back into his being. The soldier shakes his hand, introduces himself and asks him to share what he has experienced. After the briefest of summaries, the soldier asks if Stephen feels strong enough to show them around the camp. Stephen replies with a solemn nod.

Meanwhile, skeletal figures crowd around the Americans, an outpouring of gratitude and cries for water. Those who no longer have the strength to walk, crawl towards the jeep. The soldiers are overwhelmed at the situation. Naively, one soldier offers a spindly, skeletal man a cigarette and is mortified when he desperately stuffs it in his mouth and eats it. The poor souls – the men, women and children who have survived the place they were sent to die in – are in dire need of help. The Americans call for back-up. Food, water and medical aid are on their way, and they try to communicate this to the desperate and the dying. For many, help simply arrives too late. Some of those who hung on to life in the hope of liberation collapse at the sight of it and die before the eyes of the American soldiers. Others, delirious from starvation and the horrors inflicted upon them, refuse to wait for medical aid and try to jog away from the camp, only to collapse and die by the roadside.

Seeing the failed attempts at communication and the flicker of panic in the soldiers' eyes, as they fear they might lose the trust and patience of the crowd, a prisoner approaches the soldier who had introduced himself to Stephen and asks if he can get on the jeep to address the crowd, to translate the news into Hungarian. The soldier agrees and helps his skinny frame climb onto the vehicle. On the jeep, the survivor transforms – no longer a prisoner, but a political leader of sorts, calming and guiding the crowd, informing them in their mother tongue that help is on the way and that they should stay put and clear the roads for the Americans to get through. As the crowd obeys, the soldier turns back to face Stephen. In a friendly yet severe tone, he instructs: 'You're the camp commander now . . . I have two hundred German prisoners here with me – instruct them to clear the camp, burn the huts and bury the dead.'

. . . and there were many dead, Stephen adds after a heavy pause in his narration. *It was all filth and dirt and lice.*

Stephen rises to the occasion and gives orders to the German prisoners. It takes a good while to clean up and close down the camp, but much like the rest of his account of the darkest chapter in his life, he does not go into detail, nor does he express how it felt to experience this extraordinary turning of the tables.

It remains a mystery to me how Stephen is able to hold on to his strength throughout all of this. I imagine it is a good dose of adrenalin, pride and the knowledge that he is not far from finally returning home that keep his body and mind from crumbling.

I know the captain's name, not because Stephen remembers it, but because I find his own account of the liberation of Gunskirchen. What I feel as I read it is akin to euphoria – he references Stephen, a man who speaks excellent English and who helps show them around the camp.

The collection of eyewitness accounts of the liberation of Gunskirchen describe some of the terrible details that Stephen is unable to share. The Foreword by General Willard G. Wyman reads:

The damning evidence against the Nazi war criminals found at Gunskirchen Lager is being recorded in this booklet in the hope that the lessons learned in Germany will not soon be forgotten by the democratic nations or the individual men who fought to wipe out a government built on hate, greed, race myths and murder. This is a true record. I saw Gunskirchen Lager myself before the 71st Division had initiated its merciful task of liberation. The horror of Gunskirchen must not be repeated. A permanent, honest record of the crimes committed there will serve to remind all of us in future years that the freedom and privileges we enjoy in a democratic nation must be jealously guarded and protected.

Another eyewitness, Major Cameron Coffman, describes what he saw upon arrival at the camp:

A little girl, doubled with the gnawing pains of starvation, cried pitifully for help. A dead man was rotting beside her. An English-speaking Jew from Ohio hummed, 'The Yanks Are Coming', then broke out crying. A Jewish rabbi tripped over a dead body as he scurried toward me with strength he must have been saving for the arrival of the American forces. He kissed the back of my gloved hand and clutched my sleeve with a talon-like grip as he lifted his face toward heaven. I could not understand what he said, but it was a prayer. I did not have to understand his spoken word.

Our wrongdoings leave scars upon the earth, but even they grow over in time. I look at photographs of Mauthausen then and now and, while the site is being preserved as a museum, a necessary reminder of us at our worst, nature is reclaiming it. Grass is growing on the ground upon which thousands were murdered and brutally stripped of their humanity. I look at photographs of Gunskirchen – the sun shining through a tree-lined path. It is a dissonant chord – the beautiful arrogance of nature, covering up all our suffering. The commemorative plaque hammered on to stone doesn't feel worthy of the magnitude of the horrors that occurred here.

Roughly twenty thousand prisoners passed through Gunskirchen alone. The vast majority of them were Hungary's Jewish elite – doctors, professors, religious leaders, artists and writers. It is estimated that roughly six thousand Jews died on the death marches from Mauthausen to Gunskirchen. Out of the one hundred and ninety thousand held at Mauthausen concentration camp, at least ninety thousand were murdered. An estimated six million Jews were murdered in total during the Holocaust.

PART THREE

Hope

CHAPTER 17

I'd Rather Go Back to Hungary

The Americans were very friendly, they invited me to have meals with them. Of course, nobody knew the state of starvation I was in. They offered me food which was very heavy to digest. But I was eating it, not knowing the consequences.

Stephen and the other survivors are taken to a nearby town to receive first aid. The American soldiers mean well by rewarding him for his efforts with a hearty meal of American food.

Over the following days he stays with the 71st Division, volunteering to help. The American soldiers take a liking to Stephen. They provide him with temporary accommodation, food, drink and a jeep, in which he runs errands for them.

One day, he is tasked with taking fresh clothing to the hospital for the survivors. A soldier loads them into the jeep and gives Stephen a friendly pat on his bony shoulder before disappearing back into their makeshift offices. Stephen drives the short distance, feeling free and full of purpose. Having made his delivery, he decides to go for a walk before climbing back into the jeep. Reaching a square, Stephen notices just how unscathed the village nucleus is – the neat cobblestone pattern of the roads, the flower baskets hanging outside ornate window frames, an octagonal fountain in the middle of the square. A strange feeling sets in. Something about the peace and quiet fills Stephen with unease. For a moment, he stands quite still, taking in his surroundings and listening to the soft chirp of birds in nearby trees. And then he hears a different sound, a loud clang, followed by a low mumbling of voices, one of which, he is sure, sounds Hungarian. The noise seems to be coming from the otherwise dark and empty-looking church on the opposite side of the square, its heavy wooden door standing slightly ajar. Stephen acts on instinct, approaching the church with a speedy confidence. He peers into the darkness. As Stephen carefully pushes the door open, a beam of sunlight floods the aisle and pews. Hiding in a pathetic huddle behind the pulpit, Stephen sees the commanding officer of Gunskirchen and a couple of Hungarian Nazi officers.

Without uttering a word, Stephen backs out of the church, jumps in his jeep, and speeds back to denounce them to the Americans.

I only know they were arrested . . . I don't know the rest of it, I don't know what happened.

I look up who was in charge of the camp at the time of its liberation. On an Austrian website on Mauthausen, I read that Karl Schulz is camp commander – the website translates his official title as Chief Assault Leader, which seems an apt description. Of course, I am full of preconception, but when I see a photograph of his face, I shudder – with heavy-set eyes and dark, slicked-back hair, he looks like a man with a mean bite. In the Jewish Virtual Library, I find a court document dating from 1948 that mentions him, accusing him of crimes against humanity, but proposing a mere five years in prison, commencing on 8 May 1945. A quick search reveals that Schulz lived a long life as a mostly free man and a decorated war veteran. Deputy commander at Gunskirchen is Heinrich Häger. Looking at his photo, I see a man with a glint of fear in his eyes. I can picture him cowering in a pew. Heinrich Häger was caught and sent to trial within a time frame that suggests it could have been him whom Stephen discovered that day. He was sentenced to death by the American Military Tribunal in Dachau and was executed two years later. The third person listed as being in charge of Gunskirchen at the time of its liberation is Dr Hermann Richter, the camp's physician. Richter committed the most inhumane of crimes, singlehandedly murdering hundreds. It is assumed that he committed suicide near Linz that same month. It is conceivable that it could have been him behind the pulpit. Panicked by the looming consequences of his actions, he may have decided to take matters into his own hands.

I hadn't heard from my family for a long, long time, it was probably more than a year. I don't know whether they survived or not or what happened.

The following day, Stephen is called into the office at the Americans' headquarters. Behind the desk sits a large, jovial man in uniform. In a friendly and booming voice, he gestures to the chair opposite his and invites Stephen to sit.

'Listen, Stephen, if you want US citizenship, you got it!'

He leans back in his chair and takes a moment to realise that this news, while well intentioned, does not garner the expected jubilance. In a bid to excite Stephen, the lieutenant leans forward again, explaining that: 'You can catch a plane any day you want – from Paris, straight to New York. We can arrange for an escort to the airport for you, no problem!'

Stephen utters a quiet thank you. The lieutenant laughs.

'You want to go back to Hungary, don't you?'

Grateful that he will not have to explain himself any further, Stephen sighs with relief and says in a slow and deliberate tone: 'I have to go home and find my family.'

This is met with a silent understanding. The lieutenant, eager to do something for Stephen, looks off into the distance for a moment before slamming his hands on the table.

'I'll tell you what, Stephen, you get together a group of people – anyone you know and like and is fit to go home – and I'll get you a ride home.'

Like an excited child, he quickly adds: 'We'll load it up with supplies . . . anything you may need or want – cigarettes, maybe some nice booze? We'll make sure you get home, Stephen, don't you worry.'

I told this man, this officer, that I'd rather go back to Hungary.

Later the same day, Stephen and fourteen fellow survivors gather outside to meet the lieutenant. Before them stands a large, empty water tank. With a wide smile, the lieutenant walks Stephen around to the back of it. The tank is pulling a van, filled to the brim with sugar, flour, cigarettes and coffee.

'That should keep you out of trouble for a while,' the lieutenant laughs and points to different boxes stacked up in the van. After a flurry of thank-yous from everyone, Stephen turns to the lieutenant.

'Speaking of trouble . . .' He lowers his voice. 'What about the Russians?'

'Oh, they shouldn't give you any problems. You'll be all right; there's nothing to fear. I've got all your papers, refugee papers, ready for you, by the way.'

Everyone, Stephen included, is still marvelling at the van with all its glorious contents. The excitement for their imminent home-bound journey is palpable.

'So, you can all make yourselves comfortable in the van – there's one more car for you to ride alongside the van.' He turns on the spot and points towards the car.

Stephen addresses the lieutenant, eyes glinting, and declares: 'I'm going to sit on top of the water tank!'

The lieutenant looks at him, his brow scrunched in a lack of comprehension.

'You know . . . return to Hungary in triumph!'

Stephen pumps his fists in the air comically. The lieutenant lets out a belly laugh and stretches out his arms to say goodbye.

'It's only four hundred kilometres – what could go wrong? I'm getting on the tank . . .'

So I did! the older Stephen tells me in the tapes.

I wish the story would end here. It would be befitting of the closing scene of one of Julie and Richard's childhood cinema visits, the hero riding out of frame, a clenched fist above his head, into the sunset. But of course, Stephen's journey never did take him to Hollywood.

CHAPTER 18

A Room With No Walls

As they cross the river along the south-east of Austria, they are stopped by Russian soldiers. The sight of Stephen on top of the water tank surely was reason enough to inspect their company. They order everyone out of the cars.

'Get off! Get off!' a guard shouts, motioning to Stephen, who slides off the tank and joins the other crestfallen men. A flurry of angry shouts, first in Russian, then in heavily accented English: 'Papers! Give me your papers!'

Stephen hands over everything – his American visa, the letter written by the American commanding officer, his refugee papers – the Russian guards don't even look at them. Instead, they rip them to pieces. The men are ordered to line up. As the soldiers turn to rummage through their cargo, Stephen exchanges panicked glances with the others – a quiet promise to one another that they will not be captured.

On the tapes, Stephen's voice is agitated:

They drove the van away, tore all our papers up and made us march in military formation for some unknown destination.

There's a long, suspenseful pause as the tape still rolls, dragging out the unknown.

Seizing the moment when the Russian soldiers are distracted by the contraband, the men start to run. They split up, escaping as fast as their tired bodies will allow. When Stephen's voice returns on the tape, it is emphatic:

The fact remains that I escaped with the others NINE TIMES between the place where we crossed the river and Vienna, where I have arrived, I don't know how many days later. We had to walk, of course.

I pause the tape to think on what Stephen is saying and can't help but picture the scene as rather cartoonish – a ludicrous game of cat and mouse. I imagine that, in reality, the soldiers who stopped to arrest Stephen and the gang of refugees will have soon given up on the chase. The traumatic encounter will have been a shock and a hard lesson that refugee papers are no guarantee for safe passage and that, although the war is officially over, attitudes, aggression and injustice do not end overnight. Stephen and his fellow escapees will have been rightfully wary of any uniformed person they encounter on their onerous walk to Vienna. The nine escapes will most likely have been nine run-ins or near-misses with soldiers as they navigated through Russian-occupied territory.

Stephen feels safer when they finally reach Vienna, although it, too, is occupied by Russia. They walk through Austria's capital, piles of rubble lining the streets and a layer of black soot coating recently bombed areas, finally seeking help in a refugee centre. The authorities put them up in a hotel and set things in motion for them to receive new refugee papers.

This jumps out at me. Providing refugees with temporary accommodation is a hot topic in the UK as I am writing this book. I watch the news and see almost daily features on how much taxpayers' money goes towards putting up refugees in hotels and how it puts British people out of business. It is a vile narrative, framed carefully by those in power to detract from their shortcomings and ineptitude. Their inhumane policies stoke the flames of an age-old fire. Only two generations on, I am reading the same propaganda, hearing the same rhetoric and seeing the same racist torch held up by the general public as my grandfather did in his lifetime. We know what it leads to and yet, we somehow collectively choose to ignore all the signs and head down the same, dark spiral.

Stephen is lying on the single bed in his hotel room. He notices a familiar tight sensation around his ankles and looks down to see his feet swelling up. Perhaps the walk to Vienna, he thinks, was just too much for his weakened body. He suddenly feels light-headed and breaks out in a cold sweat. He closes his eyes and falls into a deep sleep. Stephen rests for a few days until he regains just enough strength to continue his journey. He is given his new refugee papers, stating clearly in both Russian and German that he is a returnee from a concentration camp.

So I took courage and left Vienna.

Stephen boards the train to Budapest. From his recollection, it seems as though he travels alone. The other survivors may already have mustered up the strength for their homebound journeys. He dares not relax a single muscle. Around him, the world whirls past, a post-war chaos, an underlying threat of anarchy and aggression heavy in the air. Russian soldiers are still arresting Austrians and Germans, taking them as prisoners of war. To Stephen, staring out of the train window, it looks as though they are taking people at random. At every stop, he sees soldiers assaulting women and girls, claiming them, too, as prisoners. He witnesses several captives surreptitiously drop scrunched-up pieces of paper on the floor – clues left for loved ones, informing them that they have been taken. It makes him think of his own family. The closer he gets to home, the more anxious he feels at the thought of what awaits him there, what fate may have befallen them. Stephen sinks into his seat, breathes in and settles down. He tries to draw as little attention to himself as possible as the train pulls out of yet another platform and moves onwards.

The journey to Budapest, Stephen says, *I had no adventure, so to speak. I arrived in an ordinary way.*

In Budapest, Stephen heads straight to the authorities, to an office that specialises in keeping track of its citizens during the war. He is so consumed by worry for his family and the need to find out what's happened to them, he doesn't fully take in the destruction around him. Arriving at the office, he states his name and is registered as 'alive and returned'. It takes all of his strength to muster up the courage to ask about his family.

'Oh yes, they have been searching for you everywhere, calling in almost every day. They are all well and alive.'

Resolve. When a melody hits the root note after gallivanting around the scale, we feel a sense of peace. We feel home. A profusion of thank-yous flows from Stephen, aimed at no one in particular. The civil servant, all too accustomed to being the bearer of news – both good and bad – and receiver of visceral reactions, simply smiles and says encouragingly: 'You're very lucky.'

Stephen is nearly out of the door when the civil servant, who had turned back to peruse the files, looks up and calls after him: 'Sir, don't go to your parents' apartment in St Stephen's Square – that's been heavily damaged. Your family are currently residing at your sister's apartment. Go there.'

The positive news is so overwhelming that it takes Stephen a while to realise that he has completely lost his bearings. His feet have carried him on instinct towards the Danube, but as he gets closer to the river, the level of destruction surrounding him is disorientating. In his absence, the city has been torn apart by conflict. The fifty-day siege of Budapest, which ceased just three months prior to Stephen's return, had been brutal and had cost hundreds of thousands of lives. Confused, he walks down streets littered with debris and past row upon row of destroyed buildings along the Danube. He reaches the point at which a crossing once was, only to see the remnants of a bridge half submerged in the murky water, with what appear to be bloated dead bodies floating around the limply hanging suspension cables.

All seven bridges connecting the city's two halves have been destroyed in battle. After German-occupied Hungary finally surrendered, Russian soldiers conscripted Hungarian men of military age to build a makeshift pontoon bridge to reunite Buda and Pest. Stephen crosses it, carefully placing one foot in front of the other, until he finally steps on to the left bank of the Danube.

The walk to Annie's apartment takes him past St Stephen's Square and he cannot refrain from taking a look at the damage. The first thing he sees is a roofless St Stephen's Basilica, its walls and towers badly damaged. He turns to his right to face his parents' apartment block and looks upward. The entire wall facing the street is missing, displaying its insides like a burnt doll's house to everyone who passes. The walls are blackened with ash and any belongings left inside that hadn't been stolen before the bombs fell have been burnt or destroyed . . . except for one thing. There it is in the far left-hand corner: the Blüthner baby grand piano, unscathed, sitting defiantly, glistening among the rubble, smiling at its owner's return.

The sight was quite funny to have a room with no walls, just the Blüthner piano standing on its own in one corner.

Stephen lets out an involuntary laugh at the beautiful absurdity of it all. In this moment, he doesn't feel the weakness of his withered muscles or the tightness around his swollen legs. He feels nothing but pure, unbridled joy and takes pride in the realisation that his beloved piano is evidently just as stoic as its player.

She opened the door and saw me. Of course, the joy turned into a fright.
Stephen arrives at Annie's apartment block. The front door is open and he walks, slowly and deliberately, up the stairs. He reaches the double wooden front door and knocks. Annie opens the door, her newborn baby Judit in her arms. She gasps at the sight of her brother. A chorus of the endearment version of his name – 'Pista!' – ricochets through the apartment, from Annie to Katica and Aladar, who are sitting in the dining room behind her. They jump up and run towards the door. Stephen takes one step over the threshold and collapses.

CHAPTER 19

All Together

I didn't get to know Stephen, but I hold my grandmother Edith in my memory. I know what it felt like to be in her warm, elegant presence. Her hair was always set in perfect, silver waves and she was always exquisitely dressed. Even as a small child, her impeccable manners and sense of style made a lasting impression. She was utterly charming and had the most delightful, girlish laugh.

Although she was never anything but pleasant, she sometimes seemed overwhelmed in the presence of small children – me and my cousin rolling around underneath the Blüthner piano proved stress-inducing for her. She would shine around the dinner table, presenting her deliciously rich, Hungarian home cooking, trying to teach an uninterested six-year-old me the correct way to cut toast.

Like Stephen, she spoke English with a thick, Hungarian accent. Hers was sweet and songbird-like. Occasionally, she'd express herself in Hungarian, involuntary phrases falling amid the immigrant English. I remember her clutching her pretty, oval-shaped face, exclaiming: 'O Istanem!' (Oh my God!)

Ten years ago, my parents found a document – a typed letter, written by Edith. I remember vividly gathering around in reverence, forming a cosy circle on the living-room floor over Christmas: me, my mum, dad and sister. It was an incredibly moving experience, reading together my grandmother's first-hand account of the horrors my family had been through.

The lengthy letter is written to her brother, who had settled in England after studying in Leeds, missing the war back home. Written on 10 March 1946, Edith's shock and grief are raw, which makes her ability to recount the horrors so eloquently and, in part, poetically, all the more remarkable.

Reading the letter was painful then, but now that I have lived more of a life, have experienced grief and am all too aware of the horrific, historical context of her words, it hurts my head as much as my heart.

I share Edith's letter almost in full. It is too rich in detail and too poignant to omit. This is her story and that of Laslo, her children Elizabeth and Peter (whom she refers to by their respective Hungarian nicknames Muci and Pistike) and her family. Its purpose becomes abundantly clear towards the end – Edith writes this letter to ask for help getting her and her family out of Hungary.

My dearest brother,

I was glad to read your letter dated February 12th, from which I understand that, at long last, you received a letter from me. The three parcels containing medicines arrived as well, for which many thanks.

It is a thrill for us to know that you did not suffer and that you did not have to endure the same horrors as was our lot, life has spared you all this, God helped you and everything worked out for you according to your plans. You cannot possibly imagine how proud we are of you, for having been able to create your future and organise your life in a foreign country without any help or assistance.

I now would like to describe to you all that happened to us since we parted; it won't be easy, but I shall try. When the war broke out, we had our worries and forebodings, but we were not really afraid, we knew we were young and hoped that God would help us.

Laci was called up in September 1940. He was serving in Transylvania for three months; I was managing the business during his absence. This meant no great hardship for me, because I had learned the routine and understood the business to a certain extent, since I had been in the shop constantly. Laci got out of the army in December and everything continued normally. However, by that time the anti-Jewish tendency started taking shape seriously and one strict decree was promulgated after the other. In August 1941, our qualification as textile wholesalers was taken away, in spite of all our petitions and all the fight we put up. This meant that our stock was seized from one hour to the next. They took possession of it and passed it over to Christian wholesalers at prices much below its actual valuation. I cannot possibly describe to you what severe loss this meant to us financially. This was the first big slap in the face for the simple reason that we were Jewish. It meant the end of textiles for us. We were left with braidings, drapery and rugs. In these, for the time being, we could still deal since they were not touched by the regulations. You can imagine how difficult it was for Laci to switch over the entire business from one day to the next. But he would not have been Laslo Somogyi had he gotten afraid. He worked more than ever, and business expanded. It was as if God would have intended to take care of us in advance, so that we will have something to live on during the next four to five years. But I do not want to forestall events. Whatever was nice in my life came to an end. Dearest, I was very happy; the children developed beautifully, Laci worked successfully, we had a lovely home and Father was proud of us, because we could live so well. Who needs bigger happiness? Nobody does, right? I had everything. And I always prayed to God not to deprive me of this beautiful happy life.

He was called up again and on the 26th of November, they escorted him to death. We were most aware already then that he who is taken out there will not return. This was no secret. The aim obviously was to exterminate the Jews. My calvary started when I last saw him in the wagon as they took him away. It was horrifying. And I cannot describe to you how much I suffered at the beginning. But in spite of everything I had hope, because he was so strong and because he so solemnly promised to me that he will come back even if he has to cross China. These were his words, and I can hear them to this day.

Thereafter, work was my only pleasure, apart from the children of course. I buried myself into the business and wanted to prove that I can stand my ground. I wanted to prove worthy of Laci so that he may be proud of me when, with God's help, he will come back home. I worked an awful lot and everything went on the same way as if he had been around. Father was very proud of me. And people could not stop being amazed that I was able to conduct that big, important business. At that time, business still was important and serious. Of course, this was not as easy a task as people believed it to be – I was without any help and or support. Dearest, please take this as I say it: I had no help or support. There was nobody next to me from whom I have got any advice.

In 1943, the fronts crumbled completely and I started worrying for Laci greatly, because I had no news whatsoever from him since January. At that time, I sent you a telegram asking that you try to investigate about him, but already then, I felt that he may have become a prisoner.

This is how the year 1943 came to pass in sadness. Alas, how these worries got dwarfed during the years to follow. Never would I have believed that I may have a deeper pain and worry than the fact that

Laci is not by my side! But this is exactly what happened. As you know, on March 19th 1944, the Germans invaded us, and this marked the end of a secure, calm life, and we lost our personal freedom. Dearest, I shall never be able to tell you and you will never be able to grasp (thank God!) what it means to live under German hegemony. Only those who were involved can measure up the terrible fright and suffering we went through. And an outsider, even when having heard about it all, cannot possibly judge the situation. So the suffering started then and there – every day brought new regulations, which gradually deprived us of all our belongings. It started with the business last April: we had to shut the premises and leave behind the entire stock, such as it was. You can probably imagine how painful this was for me. The beautiful work and its result was annihilated and turned into nothing.

What I missed most was the work itself. It was terrible to get up in the morning and not go to work, but sit at home, locked up, because after the decree concerning the wearing of the yellow star, another decree was promulgated, restricting going out. This meant that one was permitted to walk in the streets only between 11 a.m. and 2 p.m. Even the two children had to wear the star, because they were over the age of six. This was followed by regulations concerning the apartments. Certain houses were designated as 'Jewish dwellings'. The buildings themselves had to be marked with a star. Fortunately, Falk Miksa Street 12, where we lived at the time, was made one of those star houses. Because I had a four-room flat, I had to accept three more families to come live with us – ten to twelve people lived in each room. It was dreadful. It was probably the mildest of the tortures, but at the time, it proved to be the most difficult to endure and the most nerve-racking.

Meanwhile, summer arrived and we were living in complete uncertainty, not knowing what actually is in store for us. At that time, the deportation of Jews from the provinces had started already, and we learned with trepidation that our relatives and acquaintances were taken to Germany. Seventy to eighty people locked in one railway car: what their fate would be thereafter, we did not know at the time. We realised that, unless some miracle does save us, the same fate will befall us too and we were desperately trying to figure out – grasping every blade of straw, figuratively speaking – just how we could save our bare lives.

There were those who acquired false personal documents and went into hiding. This was not an easy undertaking either. It was risky living since, in case someone recognised them or found them suspicious, they would be denounced, which would mean the end. Although the risk was great, it was worthwhile, because there was pretty little hope that one could win the game in an honest way. I was constantly racking my brain as to how I could protect the children, so that they at least can stay alive. At that time, I was still hoping that with God's help Laci will return at the end of the war and can find them. At that particular time the situation was such that – provided Laci was imprisoned – he was probably in the best position. And of course you, my darling, we were thinking of you longingly, how fortunate it was that you were out there, not knowing of anything. And that at least, you will be the only survivor of the entire family.

After serious scrutiny, I decided to send the children to the provinces with false papers. I secured Christian papers for them for money. I taught them their new names. They were so clever and grasped the situation so well, that my task was not too difficult.

Uncle recommended someone who was willing to take them in for money. It was a very hard decision for me, but since I had no other choice, I went ahead and parted with them with a bleeding heart. I figured that in a village, in the fresh air, they will be far better off than being locked up in a room, that they will have better nourishment and, what is most important, that they will have a chance to survive. Unfortunately, I could not go with them, because my features would have created suspicion. The local gendarmerie, who were watching out for everyone who seemed the least bit suspicious, would have detected the Jewish descent and I thus would have caused trouble for the children. They themselves do not look Jewish at all, and hopefully God will protect them.

I parted with them in June and started working in and moved to a factory, which was designated a war enterprise. Father, Mother, Uncle and Aunty were there as well. We all thought that this was the most secure refuge for the moment. Would you want to know what I did in that factory? Imagine, I worked in the kitchen! Aunty was the head cook and I myself, together with four other kitchen maids, helped her. Regular military severity and discipline reigned there. We lived in common quarters and slept on straw sacks. We were locked up, just like in military barracks. Cooking was done for seventy people, workers and leaders. Father and Uncle were employees, just as ourselves, with the sole difference that they had separate sleeping quarters – four to a room. Sometimes, undetected, we slipped up to their place and in secret ate a few better bites, which was smuggled in for Father and Uncle to the factory. But this relatively quiet life did not last long, because when the first Jews of Budapest were gathered and deported in railway cars, we became very frightened. With permission of the head of the workshop, we all left the factory. This was our good fortune since a few weeks later all the Jewish workers and their Jewish superiors at the factory were deported.

The summer of 1944 ended with a lot of trepidation. The children had to be brought back to me, because they were in danger. The gendarmes examined my Pistike and things became suspicious. They had to be helped to flee to avoid the gendarmes and you can imagine what I went through emotionally until I had the children by my side again. At that time, I lived with my mother and, had she not been with me, I would have very likely gone crazy. All this time, we lived through horrible air-raids. I don't think I have to elaborate here about this, since you out there had similar experiences. There were days when we had four to five raids, entire rows of buildings collapsed as a result.

The sufferings did not end. And now I have to come to our financial status. We had to surrender all our jewellery and all valuables or at least declare them all. For example, as I had mentioned before, the business was seized together with the entire stock, buildings, and everything – it all had to be declared, which meant that one could not touch anything and certainly not sell anything. What actually had we been living on for more than half a year? I had a bit of money hidden away with one of my Christian employees, and he brought me some money whenever I needed funds. Furthermore, the bank where the business account had been kept was entitled to pay a very small amount per month from a 'frozen' account just so that we will not starve. Furthermore, I placed the majority of my jewellery with various friends and acquaintances and whenever I had to face a bigger expense, I covered it by selling something.

And then, October 15th came upon us. What had happened before was child's play and a festivity compared to what was in store for us thereafter. Believe me, all we had gone through was horrible enough, but you must realise that even bad things can get worse. October 15th was the day when Hungary intended to surrender. Horthy declared that we shall not fight any longer, that the Germans misguided us, the Russians reached our borders, we cannot possibly fight them and Germany does not offer sufficient help. Therefore, we are willing to dispose of arms. How happy we were – oh my God, we believed all our suffering over the war was at its end, at least for us. But unfortunately, this was not the case. How disappointed we were, how horrible it was to be informed over the radio that the Germans passed over the power and the leadership to the Arrow Cross, for them to continue the fight. This is how the entire country was ruined, deprived and robbed of everything, whilst the Jews, those few who were still around – in the provinces there were no Jews left and only a handful who lived in Pest – were deported or simply killed. Now there started a race for life. We were running hither and thither like pursued wild animals. We did not know just what to do. A few buildings were designated as sheltered houses for Jews with foreign safe papers. We were in possession of such a document and we tried to find accommodation in one of those buildings. So many of us were thrown together that there were thirty-five to forty people per apartment. Father procured for us three of the Swiss safe papers. This was the name of the document which was issued by foreign embassies. Mother did not have one yet and I got her one overnight for a golden box, because these could be obtained only for money or jewellery. This way I could take Mother with me whilst the children were taken care of by the Red Cross. Pistike was taken to a boys' institute, the Collegium Josefium, while Muci was sheltered with nuns at the Convent of the Mercy. This way I hoped to save their lives. I never trusted for a moment that we in the sheltered accommodations would be spared. This seemed a transitory stage and we had to wait and see what follows. Forty of us lived in that sheltered house in a three-room flat, and we were trembling, awaiting future developments. Mother was in care of the kitchen. We cooked together for everybody. Mother organised everything very well. This was our only activity and this is how we spent all our time.

I used to have an extremely decent helper in our business. He was an honest, reliable, simple, Christian man, father of two children, and he helped me a great deal, always provided us with food, even at the time when it was already forbidden for us to have contact with Christians. This helper of mine by the name of Jeno came to see me daily. He constantly said that he will provide me with Christian documents and that I will have to go into hiding since I have to be saved for the sake of my two children. I have to stay alive, because Laci will return and he must find us amongst the survivors. He loved Laci and wanted to save us all, at all cost. I did not have too much faith in his suggestions and was not courageous enough to go into the proposed dangerous game. But gradually I realised that he was right and that there is no other solution for me than to follow his advice. A few days later, he brought me the papers of his own sister, the marriage certificate of his own parents, and the baptismal certificate of his parents, which were all excellent documents. The best one could possibly obtain. I did not know what to do. Uncle had a Christian sister-in-law, who accepted that I live with her as a tenant under my pseudonym. And since everything was well prepared, there was nothing left for me to do than to muster enough energy and go into hiding. On the evening of December 1st, I stealthily fled from the sheltered house where I had been living for two weeks. Not even

Mother knew about it. She had happened to be in the kitchen preparing supper. I still heard her voice as I was slipping out of the corridor: 'Edith, Edith, where is that child? Has anyone seen her?' These were the last words I heard from her. It was awful. I almost burst out crying. But I could not possibly go and take leave from her because others would have noticed and my plan would have fallen through. This was how I left her. And at that moment I did not realise that I shall never see her again. Very often, when I remember this, I'm full of remorse and accuse myself, thinking that had I not left her then the poor soul would probably still be alive and would not have been taken away. That I was the cause of her misfortune. But then again, I think that God's intentions are imponderable and that who knows whether we would have survived had I stayed. This much is certain: she did know about my plan and she always encouraged me to go for the sake of the children without worrying about her, because she would not stay there anyway. Grandma and family were living in a sheltered house at number 6 Tatra Street and she intended to move there. We ourselves were not far from them. But prior to coming to Mother's tragedy, I have to tell you what happened to the Jews while we were in the sheltered house, and even before we moved there. A few days after the Arrow Cross gang came to power i.e. after October 15th, all men between the ages of sixteen and sixty-five were collected from the Jewish houses. I mentioned before that Jews had to live in special houses marked with a yellow star. Thus it was not difficult to find them and herd them together. Of course, they could only take those who were still around, since most age groups, mainly eighteen to forty or even fifty, had been called up earlier. They were taken partly to the Russian front in 1942 and later, they had to do compulsory labour in Hungary. They took away even those who happen to have returned. In other words, they took all menfolk away in railway cars and many of them on foot. They all were taken out of the country. They then reached the Nazi death camps, and the majority of them perished there. The next step concerned women between the ages of eighteen and forty. Everybody had to go and the fact that I was left out can solely be described as a stroke of luck. It would be too lengthy to give you all details. Suffice it to say that these unfortunate women were dragged out of the country as well, partly on foot, partly squeezed into railway cars, same as the men. Their destinations were the German death camps, too. You may have heard about them.

Ninety per cent of the Jewish population was dragged away in October/November. A few of us who lived in sheltered houses escaped the worst for the time being. But the Arrow Cross gangsters were still not satisfied. Once we had already congregated in the sheltered house, they started to vacate those and dragged away people one after the other. Some were taken to the ghetto. By that time, the ghetto had already been installed; it was located between Kiraly Street, Karoly Ring, Erzsebet Ring and Dohany Street. This territory was designated to be the ghetto: those who were still home and were not living in sheltered houses had to move there. These were mostly old folks and all those who by chance were left out of the masses that were dragged away. When I saw that living in a sheltered house means no protection, I decided to leave but I thought I would somehow get a hold of papers and accommodation for Mother as well, so that I can put her into hiding too. But after I had left, Mother had no will to stay. She wanted to join Grandma at all costs. And when a few days later, I sent Aunty Jolan to her (this was the Christian sister-in-law of Uncle, with whom I lived by then), Mother persuaded her to accompany her to number 6 Tatra Street to Grandma's. She packed her rucksack marked with the yellow star. And this proved fatal. She started out to join Grandma; Aunt Jolan accompanied her because Mother was very short-sighted, and in those days it was most danger-ous to walk in the streets since the Arrow Cross gangs grabbed every-body and either threw them into the ghetto or worse. Later on, when deportation became impossible because the Russians closed the fron-tiers, people were herded and tied together in the streets and simply thrown into the river Danube. This fate befell Bela Bodor and Teri. Thus Mother started off with Aunt Jolan to proceed to Grandma's, but when she reached the gate, she remembered having forgotten her overshoes upstairs and sent Aunt Jolan back up to fetch them. She said she herself would meanwhile go ahead slowly so that Aunt Jolan could catch up with her. But when Aunt Jolan reached downstairs again Mother was nowhere to be found. She looked for her every-where. She ran to Grandma at number 6 Tatra Street, but she was not there either. As we later found out, this is what happened. Hardly had Mother taken a few steps, she ran into a group of Arrow Cross gangsters. Noticing the yellow star on Mother's rucksack, they dragged her into the ranks, stating that this is where she belonged. Dearest, it is gruesome to write about this. I suffered terribly, the thought of what she must have gone through . . . It is most painful to think about it. How much more awful must it have been to expe-rience it? This happened on December 6th, and on the 8th, they closed her up in a railway car and deported her from the country. She was first taken to Gunskirchen and from there to Bergen-Belsen, where she disappeared without leaving any trace. And up to this day we don't know anything about her. These things were relayed to me by Janice Schwartz. You may remember him – he is the youngest son of Laci's sister, who by chance found himself in the same railway car as Mother. They were together up until Gunskirchen, where they were 'distributed'. He returned home around June 1945 and it was he who told me all this, but this is all he knew. All searches proved fruitless. Nobody who managed to get back from there knows anything about her, except for a girl who says she saw her in Bergen-Belsen in February '45. She says that at that time, Mother was still relatively well – she still owned her dress and her coat. But this particular girl got taken away from the camp in February and knows no more about Mother's fate. I myself only found out all this in March 1945. When Buda was liberated, and I could come over to Pest – up until then, I thought Mother was taken to the ghetto, because nobody dared tell me anything else so that I should not get distressed even more. This was the time when I found out what had happened to Father. I did not know anything about him between December 1944 and March 1945. This was so because, since I was in hiding under a false name, I could not be in touch with anybody. Except through Jeno, my shop assistant, because according to the papers, I was his younger sister. Only he could visit me. I did no walking around so that I will not get caught. So as I mentioned before, the children were in various institutions and Jeno kept visiting them, too. And this way, I had news about them. Jeno was extremely decent. He took the children home to his family every Sunday, and it was there that the two of those poor souls could see each other. You can imagine what they suffered emotionally. They had to go through so much. They had not seen me for over four weeks by then. That is when Christmas arrived. It was Jeno's wish that Christmas can be spent together, the children and myself, and he planned to steal me over to Buda, where they lived. This was a most daring enterprise, since many Arrow Cross gangsters lived in that building. But he was adamant to do everything so that during the holidays, at least, we could be together. And he brought the children to his house and then under the cover of night, he guided me across. We made the journey, trembling and in fright. But God helped us and we made a crossing successfully. You can imagine how glad the children were and what happiness I felt to be able to see them again and spend a few hours quietly as a family. Those simple people were so good to us, that I can state bravely never to have experienced so much kindness and love than on this particular occasion. I am indebted to them for the life of my children and of my own, because just when I was over there, on the evening of December 24th, the long-awaited attack of the city started. At long last the Russians surrounded the city, and the big battle began, which lasted until February 12th. This is what we had been waiting for all along for weeks on end, because we knew that this is the only way for us to be saved. The only miracle that could help us was the Russian attack, provided the Russians got here on time. They would liberate us and then maybe there would be no time to exterminate everybody. So the attack of Buda began on Christmas Eve. It appeared then that Buda would be liberated in a matter of days. But Buda was so strongly defended by the Arrow Cross gangs, that what actually happened is what we least believed possible: Pest was liberated much earlier, on January 18th, while Buda had to suffer another month of battles fought there. The few surviving Jews are indebted for their lives to the fact that the Russians finally reached Pest and started their attack. Had the storming lasted for less time, more of us may have remained alive because there would have been less time to exterminate us. Not even during the storming could the Arrow Cross gangsters be halted and even during late December and the first days of January, many

unfortunate people lost their lives. Jeno and his family took an enormous risk by hiding us, since when Jews were found in a Christian
home, the Christian families were put to death together with their
protégés. You can well imagine that we were trembling. When the
great attack started on 24th December, it was impossible to cross
over to Pest the next day, and thus neither the children nor I myself
could be slipped back to Pest anymore. But this may have been our
good fortune. Because this way we could stay together and could live
through the horrors in each other's company. You cannot imagine
how horrible the storming proved to be. First, electricity was cut off.
Then bombardments and many direct hits at various buildings. One
had to spend most of the time in the cellar. For six weeks. We were
locked up, nine of us in that small shelter. There were four children,
two of mine and two of Jeno's wife, his sister, the latter's daughter-in-
law, a young woman and myself. After a while we had no more water.
Whenever there was a bit of calm, one had to quickly run out somewhere in the neighbourhood. Meanwhile, the bombardment started
afresh. It was horrifying. Then the reserve food ran out. This was the
worst, the poor children were very hungry. Eventually we got food
from the soldiers, sometimes from Hungarian soldiers, at another
time from German ones. All the time we lived in fright that someone
may find out that we were Jewish, but God helped us and we lived to
see the end. And on 12th February, the entire city was liberated. The
Russians had captured Buda as well. Pest, as I mentioned before, was
liberated on 18th January already. All bridges were demolished by
explosives by the Germans that night after they had crossed over to
Buda to defend that part of the city further. But all their efforts were
in vain. They were vanquished by the Russians and finally, all the
suffering came to an end. I cannot describe what I felt when after six

weeks I emerged from the cellar as a free human being and could resume being Mrs Laslo Somogyi instead of Jolan Wippner, whom I impersonated for so long. Can you fathom my feelings when I saw the sky, the sun, for the first time again and realised that I am alive, free, a human being and not a persecuted animal any longer. What I saw was awful, ruins around me everywhere. More and more ruins all around. Mud, filth, blood, corpses in the streets, which were not streets but battlefields for weeks on end. Corpses of the horses and German soldiers were lying on top of each other in the mud, but I could not care less. WE are alive. The three of us, my two children and myself, and of course, Jeno, and his family. Thank God we all escaped the worst. We were hugging and kissing one another and could not get enough of the feeling of freedom, which we had been deprived of for so long. There is no more danger. Everything is over. Now let us go and start living again.

Unfortunately, we had to stay in Jeno's flat for more than a month since there were no bridges, and it was most dangerous to cross the river by canoe. But I started to get some news from home. I learnt about Father and that my family were all right, that my place of business was completely robbed and that my apartment, although devastated by a nearby bomb explosion, was still there and that I should not worry. My family were waiting for us patiently. For them, life started again in Pest – we were told who survived, who disappeared. But there was no news to impart about Mother. This worried me a great deal. Only on the night before I was finally able to cross over, Jeno told me not to look for her, since she had been deported in December. This is the way I found out . . . You know, don't you, what I felt? She was your mother as well, but please don't begrudge me, it was I who loved her more and her loss was very, very painful for me. And as long as I live, I shall feel remorse for perhaps having sacrificed her life to save mine. I left her. Had I not done so, both of us may have stayed alive right there. As I found out later, nobody from that particular sheltered house was taken away. People either escaped the way I did or stayed there and those who did were liberated. Who could have foreseen how it would all be?

Father suffered a lot, too. I believe he wrote you that he was in hiding with Aunty in Pest. They were caught by the Arrow Cross gangsters and taken to one of their houses, where Aunty committed suicide. Father was saved miraculously, you cannot fathom what state he was in . . . When we first met, he was so weak from hunger and from being beaten that he was unable to stand on his own two feet for quite some time to come. But as time passed, and spring arrived, 'Joie de Vivre' returned. I started working again. I reopened my plundered shop where amongst lots of rubbish I found a few pieces of value, remnants of my immense stock. I started working again in my own little business, and I was free. I could go wherever I wanted, whenever the fancy took me – nobody stopped me in the streets for identification, asking why I wasn't wearing the yellow star. People started to put behind them the memory of the past and the horrors. We were looking forward to welcoming back those who had been deported. But unfortunately, very few of them came and no news reached us concerning Mother. Nothing could be found out about the prisoners either, which was a great disappointment to me. Slowly our life started to take shape again. By the end of May we had electricity again. By June, we had gas for the kitchen. The tramway circulated, they started to restore the city, which was in shambles. Only our hearts cannot find peace. Ever so many miserable people are walking the streets. It is not just me. Everybody seems affected. The husband of one, the parents of the next and the children of the third one are missing. There are so many people who were left completely alone. I have to thank God for having saved my two children and Father. But we shall never reconcile the loss of our dear mother. Are you surprised, darling, that after all the foregoing, I ask you in this, my first letter, to help us to get away from here? Can one be happy here, where every building, every street is full of sad memories? I have to walk along Tatra Street every day, and think that my poor mother was taken right here to her death. I have to see the river Danube which became the grave of so many unfortunate people who were thrown into it, and I have to live among the killers, the criminals who are walking about in freedom, as very few of them were caught and executed. Is it possible? Is it worth living here? Is it worth my while creating a new existence only for it to be taken away from me again in a few years' time? I'm sure you are not surprised that I would like to flee this place. To go to any place in the world where they will accept us, where I intend to work honestly, just as I did here, and where I can raise my children. Nothing in the world holds me here. There is not even a graveside where I could have a good cry. God alone knows where my poor mother is buried. I still don't know whether my husband is alive, or whether he too is resting in Russian soil somewhere. I don't know and I don't hope for anything, except for the possibility that with God's help, I shall get out of here. And now I shall bring this to a close. Forgive me, my dear, for the length of this report. There is a lot I left out. I could have written twice as much. Even so, I have been writing this letter for a month in at least five instalments because there is little time in my life for such pursuits. It is almost midnight. I am rather tired and I have to get up early in the morning. What I am afraid of is that this letter will be weighty and that it will not reach you. Let us hope it will though. At any rate, I wrote it in two copies, and if the first one should get lost, I shall prepare another copy. Before I finish, let me tell you that the three of you are our only joy. Every one of your letters means a holiday for us. You make me most happy when you write. So let me ask you to write frequently. We had to be silent for such a long time. Let us tell each other everything. It is such a good feeling for me to have you at least; we loved each other very much always. I was missing you so very much during the last eight and a half years, ever since you left here.

I think about Edith's mother, my poor great-grandmother Ilona, often. I learned at a young age that she died in the concentration camp of Bergen-Belsen. What haunts me is the thought of her innocence. I picture a short-sighted, well-meaning woman smiling on the street, walking straight into the arms of the Arrow Cross. Her short-sightedness was caused by a rare, hereditary eye condition. I have it too and can relate to not being able to make out whether someone approaching is friend or foe.

We had only ever had this story, never definitive proof of what happened to Ilona at the concentration camp. I remember one day, my mother was watching a documentary on the Holocaust. She jumped up from the sofa to grab the remote. With a loud exclamation of surprise, she paused the broadcast: 'Look!' she shouted, wide-eyed. On the paused screen, the camera is caught panning over a logbook of names, a list of those killed in Bergen-Belsen. There, in the middle of the alphabetised column, is her name: Reich, Ilona (Budapest).

*   *   *

Thank God our family has remained intact and we have been all together
after the war was over.

The fact that Stephen's entire family unit survived the war is nothing short of a miracle. Around the same time as he was sent to
Sopron ghetto, Lorant and George were sent to work at Budapest's
Ferihegy airport. When Germany invaded, their forced labour group
was disbanded, but en route back to their sister's apartment, where
the rest of the family were staying by now, they were arrested by the
Arrow Cross and marched to Budapest-Józsefváros train station,
from where Jewish Hungarians were being put on trains and sent to
Auschwitz.

Lorant and George were among the very lucky few who managed
to escape the train. At this stage in the conflict, philanthropist Raoul
Wallenberg and his people were trying to save as many Jewish
Hungarians from deportation as possible. They were among the
Arrow Cross soldiers at the train station, literally pulling people back
off the train before it departed. They had jurisdiction to claim
anyone who had procured safe papers. Lorant was in possession of
such papers, but George was not. The details remain unclear, but
whether it was successful pleading, persistence, sheer gall or dumb
luck, both brothers were let off the train.

After their narrow escape, Lorant and George made it to their
sister's apartment in a designated Jewish safe house on Katona Joseph
Street. Together with the other tenants of the building, the family
survived the rest of the war by huddling in the building's basement
– Katica, Aladar, Lorant, George, Annie, her husband József and
their baby Judit. Even throughout the heaviest bombings, they
needed to stay quiet and vigilant, because on occasion Arrow Cross
soldiers broke into houses to steal money, watches and anything else

that was left to take. Supplies were scarce and trips outside to scavenge for food were a huge gamble. One time, when a horse was killed by a Russian or German bomb close to the house, they took the risk. Their need for food was so great that, with kitchen knives and buckets, they ran outside and carved up pieces of the dead animal to take back and cook in the basement. Then one day there was a knock on the basement door. They opened it to see a Russian soldier who was carrying a sack across his shoulder. When he opened it to retrieve a large, dark loaf of bread and handed it to them, they knew the war was finally over.

Judit was too young to remember the tumultuous start to her life in the basement of the Jewish safe house. But as far back as her memory reaches, she has always been aware of how unusual it was that her family remained intact. Out of all the Jewish children in her school in Budapest, there was only one other whose mother and father had both survived the war. To me, it is incredible to think what turbulence Judit was born into. Coming into this world in October 1943, the first year and a half of her existence was spent fighting for survival.

During one conversation we had I remarked upon this, exclaiming: 'What a way to start life!'

'Yes,' she smiled back at me with the slightest of shrugs. 'But I *have* my life!'

And after a short pause, she concluded: 'We were very lucky.'

CHAPTER 20

What Sort of People Had We Been?

I must tell you that of course my weight was down again to 42 kilos so it happened twice in about three years that I lost my normal weight to a ridiculous few kilos.

After his collapse, Stephen is rushed to hospital. This time, his family is by his side. His condition is critical. In addition to jaundice and a high fever, he develops mysterious yellow and pink circles all over his body. At first, the doctors cannot explain them. The circles cover his abdomen and his back and vary in size, ranging from between six and twenty centimetres in diameter. Stephen sees an array of doctors in an attempt to get a diagnosis for his strange rash. It is an American doctor who finally informs him that this is a symptom of the extreme starvation Stephen suffered in the camp. The heavy, fatty foods he was given by the well-meaning soldiers immediately after liberation wreaked havoc with his system and caused a rare infection.

Stephen's youngest brother George meets with Edith soon after he is admitted to hospital and informs her of Stephen's return and of his critical condition. She starts to visit him regularly. Bound by survival, Stephen and Edith grow closer. Throughout the nine months that it takes for him to recuperate in hospital, Edith cares for him, bringing him home-cooked meals and keeping him company. They share stories, woes and, above all, a desire to start anew.

The feelings Edith develops for Stephen play out in contradiction to the grief she feels for Laslo. Her love for him is so apparent in the letter. The more she allows herself to give in to her feelings for Stephen, the less she is able to hold on to the hope that her husband might still return. Regardless, Laslo would forever be tied to them both. There is a shared anecdote in my family about this. It will have to remain just that – a story – but apparently, Laslo had said to Stephen before they parted in Russia: 'If I don't return, promise me to take care of Edith.'

Edith posts the letter to her brother before meeting Stephen at the hospital on the day of his release. I can understand why she wouldn't have mentioned their relationship. It is simply too new and too insignificant in the scheme of things – after having no contact with her brother for the duration of the war, there were too many horrors to relay, too much suffering, to tell him about a budding romance.

Parting advice from the doctors is for Stephen to eat as meat-heavy a diet as possible in order to combat the rash and continue to build his strength back up.

'If you want to have some excellent meat dishes,' Edith chirps as she locks arms with Stephen as they go for a last walk around the hospital grounds together, having overheard the doctor's advice, 'my uncle has a restaurant up in the hills! Why don't we go there together? It'll be on the house and, from memory, they even have a piano.'

'That would be nice,' he smiles.

Music and memory are intrinsically linked. A melody can reach through time and pull the listener back to when it first fell upon their ears. Sometimes songs are the only remnants we have of lost loves.

The 'Kingdom of Hungary' (or the 'Horthy era' as it's often referred to in the history books) is no more. It is dissolved and, in its stead, the Second Hungarian Republic is founded in the city of Debrecen on 1 February 1946. The new government consists of an uneasy coalition: that of the Independent Smallholders' Party and the Hungarian Communist Party. While the former had won a clear majority in the 1945 elections, in the wake of Soviet Occupation, it was insisted upon that members of the pro-Russian Communist Party take up key posts in the Cabinet. From this vantage point, the Hungarian Communist Party proceeded and continues to successfully undermine their opponents.

Stephen can't go home. His bachelor flat is occupied – a Nazi officer, sure that the owner would not return, has simply claimed it, furniture and all. With Edith's help, Stephen starts a lengthy court process to try to get it back. For now, he stays with his parents, who themselves are living in temporary accommodation, seeing as their bombed-out apartment is still uninhabitable. Within it, the Blüthner piano still sits patiently. The silver lining of this is that Stephen is much closer to Edith, who is currently living with her father in his apartment, together with her two children and a small, upright piano, just a couple of streets away.

'Go on, play it, you're very welcome,' Edith says as she notices that Stephen has stopped listening to her conversation and is eyeing up the instrument instead.

Without hesitation Stephen takes a forward step, giving her arm a small squeeze as he passes her. He pulls the piano stool towards him and sits down. With both hands, he carefully lifts the lid of the instrument and looks down at the black and white keys. He runs his thumb across the slightly weathered middle C. There's a hesitation and, for a moment, he is unsure what to play, where to start, after all this time.

Chopin, he concludes, is as good a place as any – a childhood memory waltz, to ease back into himself. He turns his head and gives Edith a smile, before positioning his hands and pressing down on the keys. He plays the 'Minute Waltz', a tune his mother taught him. She used to play the left-hand triplets while he would stretch his little fingers and play the right-hand melody as fast as he could. On this occasion, he takes his time, picking up speed as he grows in confidence.

Over the following months, Stephen spends a lot of time at this upright piano, with Edith and occasionally little Peter and Liz as audience. Over half a century later, Peter still recalls some of the melodies composed and played here, such as the love song 'A Fire Red Rose'.

Early spring in 1946 I was going to Mummy's [Edith's] shop quite regularly, just to be with her.

18 May 1946 should have been a happy day. Stephen turns thirty-nine and this year, more so than on any previous birthday, his mere existence is worthy of celebration. The day starts out just fine. The sun is out and Stephen has a spring in his step as he walks through town to pay Edith a visit in her shop. As he pushes open the front door, he pops his head around it and comically mimics the by now familiar tune of the bell. Edith sings a birthday tune as she emerges from behind the counter and dances towards him until they embrace.

'Maybe you'd like to go for a walk to the jeweller's?' she suggests.

'Now why would I do that? I've just been on a nice, long walk to see you here!'

'Yes, but . . . who knows, maybe there's a birthday present there waiting? Someone could have picked out something nice for you,' she teases.

'Someone?' He smiles. 'Well, this someone sounds enchanting, don't you think?'

'Oh yes!' she agrees.

Stephen makes his way to collect his generous birthday treat – an engraved watch – from the new and unexpected love in his life. His thoughts are so firmly with Edith that he doesn't notice two police-men starting to follow him. It's not until he's back outside Edith's shop that they stop him. After a brief exchange, they say that they want to take him in for questioning, assuring him that this is no cause for alarm. Overhearing the commotion – the low, gravelly tone of Stephen's voice does tend to travel – Edith comes rushing out of the shop. With a stern face, she addresses the police officers. 'Excuse me, what is the problem here?'

But before the final word falls out of her pursed lips, one of the police officers stretches out an arm, keeping her at a distance.

'Madam, is this your husband?' he asks without looking at Edith.

Taken aback, she lets out a little no, and the police officer barks: 'Well then, I'm afraid this doesn't concern you.'

Stephen tries to reassure Edith and says, in a calm and collected tone, 'It's okay; they're just wanting to ask me a couple of questions.'

Anxious, Edith asks the police officers how long they anticipate this will take. It is Stephen's birthday after all, she stresses, and they have plans.

'It's fine,' Stephen says naively. 'I'll only be gone a short while.'

*   *   *

I was raised to be an anti-nationalist. I know instinctively, by my war-torn family tree, that the concept of a nation state is a dangerous fiction. Growing up in Berlin around the turn of the millennium, I had never seen a proud display of German flags until Germany hosted the World Cup in 2006. The sight of them in their masses unnerved me. Some neighbours never lowered their flags after the celebrations. They move, slowly and suspiciously, in the breeze as I pass them by.

I have never seen the appeal of arbitrary lines drawn into sand. My identity has never been tied to any nation or land. I understand local patriotism, romanticising home and being a proud participant in one's community. I don't have it in me to place any value in a national pride. It's as though I carry Stephen's feelings of betrayal in my bones.

Stephen is led into an interrogation room. Facing him is a slight but fierce-looking police officer, boasting war medals on his uniform and brandishing a heavy plank of wood in his hands. The man accuses Stephen of an array of made-up crimes and threatens to beat him if he does not confess to them. Stephen recognises him – as boys they had attended the same Catholic school. Stephen stands his ground, denying the charges vehemently. His former school colleague tries to force false confessions by beating him continuously with the plank.

Stephen is arrested and thrown into a prison cell. The only sensation he feels in this moment is utter helplessness.

I can tell you that in jail I was in the best of companies, Stephen says bitterly in the tapes.

He looks around him and sees that the downtrodden faces are familiar. They belong to Jewish members of society – the few who have survived – particularly those associated with any kind of wealth or influence. Business and real estate owners, people of note and influence, are arrested, beaten and bullied into giving false confessions to various arbitrary crimes. This is a way for the government to cheat its way out of handing stolen property back to its Jewish citizens – a criminal record, however small or falsely acquired, will often be given as a reason to not grant reparation requests.

Arriving at this part of the story, a sentence I read long ago jumps to the foreground of my mind: *Emil died in a poor house in 1945.* The peculiar feeling of generational knowing sets in and I now understand how this could have happened. I picture Emil Holtzer in a similar position – beaten and crouched down in a corner of a prison cell, his business seized, his home confiscated and his son, Bela, so very far away.

It is the height of injustice that Stephen finds himself in a prison, while so many of the key orchestrators of the Holocaust have yet to be put on trial.

It is here, in the prison cell, where Stephen's heart finally breaks. Standing still, he dissociates and sees himself as a small boy, playing in his Hussar uniform. Under his breath, he recites the poems he wrote, odes to the lost territories of Hungary, at the age of ten. He remembers them all. He feels his mind reconnect with his body and takes in his surroundings, making eye contact with his brethren and exchanging knowing glances. In the tapes, Stephen's speech intensifies, his cadence building as dramatically as in one of his compositions. Even after all these years and through the ageing tape, this memory is uniquely sharp. Stephen shares exactly what is going through his mind in this very moment:

I have been brought to the position where I have to fight for my life in

Russia, then in Mauthausen and, on top of that, even the so-called new democratic government, like the Nazis, didn't tolerate people like we have been!

There's a heavy pause:

What sort of people had we been?

We have been patriotic business families. We have been cultured, art and music lovers. We have even been titled from the King of the Austrian Hungarian Monarchy. We have, of course, been law-abiding. We even converted to the Christian religion! 'Jewish' is a religion – we were always first Hungarian.

Throughout Stephen's life, his identity, above anything else, was firmly hinged on being a proud nationalist. But now, standing in the prison cell, he finally concedes. He makes a vow to leave Hungary and to never return.

This was when I really and truly decided that I will leave Hungary as soon as I can.

It is only because of the tireless efforts of Edith and Katica that Stephen is finally freed after three months' imprisonment. Eventually, they are able to persuade a lawyer to take on the case and the charges are dropped soon after. The accusers have no evidence to back up any of their claims, bringing the case to a swift close.

Around September time they set me free, all charges were dropped – it was just a matter of a little three months lost of my liberty.

Stephen finds liberation in his decision to leave. It is easier than he thinks, to shed the layer of his identity that is so firmly tied to his homeland. Over a quarter of Budapest's buildings are completely destroyed and the city is still in disarray, debris and destruction dulling the shine on the Pearl of the Danube. The city will heal, but to Stephen, the scarring would be permanent. He no longer recognises his hometown, nor does he much identify with the person he once was within it, the version of himself who felt free and happy here. It is ironic that, just as he starts to cut ties with his homeland, it in return starts to shower him with accolades and appreciation.

CHAPTER 21

Remember Me

Success often finds us the moment we stop reaching for it. Pop music history is littered with stories of musicians who let go of lofty ambition after years of hard graft, only to suddenly and unexpectedly land a hit. 'It takes ten years to become an overnight success' is a quip I have heard many times through my decade of relentless gigging.

When Stephen goes through his post and sees an official-looking letter, he eyes it suspiciously. He has grown accustomed to bad news delivered via ink on paper. On this occasion, though, the contents are met with delight. His publisher informs him that one of their biggest stars has recorded and is due to release one of his songs. In a twist of fate, 'Emlékszel Meg' ('Remember Me'), a song that Stephen wrote with Ivan Szenes back in 1941, becomes a hit.

The lyrics of the chorus are eerily prophetic:

Do you remember
how many great miracles we waited for
And how we stopped our journey halfway through,
You and I

It is akin to magic, how the meaning of lyrics can change. A great song takes a real emotion, a deeply personal experience and expresses it in such a way that it speaks a universal truth. When those words were first written, Ivan will have had his father in mind – an interrupted journey serving as a beautiful metaphor for his mentor's untimely passing. But suddenly, the words are just as true of the composer and lyricist themselves, having had all their big dreams so rudely interrupted and their lives put on hold. And now, in 1946, the words take on a new meaning once more. With hundreds of soldiers parting with war-time love affairs and a thick layer of sorrow, grief and nostalgia in the ether, 'Remember Me' becomes a zeitgeist anthem six years after it was written.

It is a thrilling sensation for Stephen, to turn the dial and to hear the romantic tune of 'Emlékszel Meg' emerge from the static. Just over a year ago, his family was by law prohibited from owning a radio and now it is his melody transmitting from it into the homes of the nation, as if it were broadcasting Stephen's very survival.

Now, they performed this piece of music and of course it was a big success. I have a record of it here with me, so that I can play it to anyone who would be interested to hear it.

I am listening to the recording of 'Emlékszel Meg'. This, the most popular version, is performed by Hungary's famous jazz singer Kató Fényes. In 1946, Fényes is a big star. She performs in the most prestigious theatres, clubs and embassies and is the first Hungarian artist to popularise songs by Frank Sinatra and Judy Garland. Fényes started her career in musical theatre as early as 1936. During the war, she and her husband saved several Jewish families from persecution by hiding them in their Budapest apartment and their house in the countryside.

Her recording of 'Emlékszel Meg' opens with a crescendo of luscious string and brass orchestration that falls and delicately curves like a wave underneath the piano and vocal. The piece is incredibly evocative – it is full of nostalgia, of longing and of romance. Her voice brings a levity and a sweetness to an otherwise mournful sentiment of the song. The dreamy, orchestral break in the middle of the song conjures up images of lovers in their finery, swaying to the music on a gilded dance floor.

In one of the tapes, Stephen does what I am doing now – recording his compositions from one medium on to another, in a bid to keep it safe for future generations. Recording shellac vinyl on to cassette, he introduces each track before playing it. Reflecting on 'Remember Me', he says:

The music is composed by me and the lyrics are written by Ivan Szenes. It was written in 1940. Just before . . . before the Holocaust.

There's something unsettling about hearing Stephen say the word. It catches me off guard and somehow sounds more poignant in his accent – the elongated vowels and threateningly silent 'h', as if the word itself is being choked – hangs heavy in the air. The sweetness of the song that follows, with its romantic orchestration and dreamy melody, is a stark contrast.

It is uncanny that the song itself is called 'Remember Me'. At times, Stephen isn't sure if he remembers himself. It is hard to remember who he was back when he composed the song. It is hard to think back on what his hopes and dreams were then. After everything he has lived through, it feels jarring to receive positive attention, to be in demand. Understandably, Stephen meets his success with distrust and a sense of vindication in equal measure as the romantic and wistful 'Remember Me' becomes a nationwide hit. He can't escape it – it's played everywhere, as if a final bid by Hungary to lure this pianist into staying.

*   *   *

'So! A French-style musical comedy!' Ivan Szenes clasps his hands together and leans back into his chair. Strewn across the table in front of him are sheets of music notation and two cups of espresso. Stephen and his songwriting partner are in a coffee shop, determined to seize the moment and work on more music.

The success of 'Emlékszel Meg' was an excellent opportunity to reconnect with Ivan – both he and his mother are well – to pick up their collaboration where they had left off. Their first meeting had been together with all the family, a joyous reunion, but not without its darker moments. Over dinner, there is much discussion in lowered tones over Ivan's cousin Hannah. Hannah Szenes, a brilliant poet in her own right, had joined anti-Nazi activist groups and fought to save Hungarian Jews from deportation to concentration camps in occupied territories. On a parachute mission in Yugoslavia, she was arrested by the Hungarian fascist Arrow Cross soldiers and tortured, but she refused to reveal details of her mission. She was put on trial for treason and executed by firing squad in November 1944.

At the coffee shop, Stephen and Ivan are revisiting one of their grander projects, the musical comedy they began writing before the war. Stephen looks down at his incomplete compositions and rests his freshly shaven chin in his hands. 'It's been so long since I've even thought about this,' he says.

He reaches for his cup. Looking around the coffee house, he takes a sip before adding in a wry tone: 'I haven't had much headspace for comedy.'

'You can't choose momentum, my friend, it chooses you!' Ivan replies with a smile. 'This is huge – we have a hit!'

Ivan breaks into song, singing the words of the chorus to 'Emlékszel Meg'.

'How could I forget? It's everywhere,' Stephen jokes.

Over the next months, Ivan and Stephen spend most of their time working on the play, finalising both the words and music in a traditional French style. Stephen promises that he will finish and perform the comedy opera with Ivan. He does not share with his friend that he is intent on leaving the country and that it'll therefore most likely be their last collaboration.

Edith's plans to emigrate are underway. With the help of her brother, she obtains the papers necessary to settle in England. During the sanctity of pillow talk, Stephen and Edith start discussing the possibility of having him join her, for them to start a new life, together.

CHAPTER 22

Sleep, Sleep, Little Boy

As the leaves on the trees wither and drop, new life is on the way. Edith is pregnant. A warmth fills me as I think of the prospect of my dad's existence as a signifier of new beginnings. The timing of it feels fated.

It is a little unclear as to whether the decision for Stephen to emigrate with Edith came before or after the news. In fact, in the tapes, Stephen doesn't mention my dad at all. Perhaps he simply didn't think to mention it – this is the story of his survival – or maybe he bowed to society's pressures, thinking that a pregnancy out of wedlock was not something one would commit to tape. Either way, around Christmas time, Stephen and Edith decide they should get married.

For her, this is no easy or straightforward feat. In order to marry Stephen, Edith needs to declare Laslo dead. The weight of this decision would lay heavy on her soul for the rest of her life. The hurt and confusion would spill over on to the two children from her first marriage.

Late in her life she would often say to my mother: 'Joj darling, what am I to do when I die? I will have two men waiting for me!'

Swept up in an icy whirlwind of events, Stephen and Edith frantically wrap up their lives in Budapest. On 8 February, my grandparents get married at the register office. It is a rushed and simple affair, with Stephen's youngest brother George and a friend of Edith's as their witnesses.

It was a bitter cold day. The flowers didn't last very long, I'm afraid. They were lilacs, I remember . . .

On their 'so-called' wedding night, as he refers to it in the tapes, Stephen performs at Budapest's Grand Opera Ball. On this night, each room within the opulent opera house is converted into a bar, a coffee shop or a restaurant, boasting live music in every venue. It is a prestigious affair – Stephen's performance is broadcast live over national radio. Among an array of his own compositions and popular songs of the day, he plays 'Emlékszel Meg', much to the delight of the enchanted audience. Edith sits alone at home, listening to her new husband on the radio.

It was an out-of-the-ordinary wedding night for both of us.

On 11 February, only three days after the wedding, my intrepid grandmother leaves the country, branching out, away from the family tree, down a new path. She leaves just in time, for in Hungary, a new tension is rising between the democratically elected government and a growing, communist movement, preparing for a coup that would herald a new chapter of unrest and violence in the already destroyed capital.

In tandem with the rise of this new threat, Stephen conducts his career along an intense crescendo of performances and compositions, soaking up every last drop of musical adventure that Budapest has to offer. Shortly after Edith's departure, Stephen and Ivan premiere their musical comedy, *Lady of Promise* (Igéret Hölgeje), at the Medgyaszay Theatre in Budapest.

It was a great success, Stephen states matter-of-factly on the tapes, before adding: *of course, it was most unfortunate that Mummy couldn't be there.*

In secret, Stephen starts work towards obtaining a passport shortly after the premiere. Weeks later, the operetta is still running and garnering rave reviews, but Stephen is preparing to leave. When other performance and recording opportunities come in over the next few months, he is evasive and non-committal.

And on the longest day of the year, Edith gives birth. In the tapes, Stephen doesn't mention how he feels when the news reaches him. But I find sheet music for a song composed by him and, as I read his hand-written lyrics, my heart swells with the fatherly love radiating from the page.

Sleep, Sleep, Little Boy
Verse and Music composed by Stephen de Bastion – Bastyai Istvan
For baby boy Richard's Birthday
'Sleep, sleep, little boy, you should dream of fun and joy.
Angels play with you at night, sleep my little child.
Dream of happy things, fairy tales and good old kings,
lots of toys to please your heart, so sleep my little child.
In the night, when it is dark, Daddy is watching you.
He will see, carefully, that all your dreams come true.
One day you'll grow up, but Daddy's love will never stop.
And in your dream this melody will make you dream of me.

CHAPTER 23

Farewell to Budapest

'Have you not told Ivan you're leaving?' Katica asks Stephen at dinner while discussing his move.

'No,' he replies, without looking up from his plate of paprikas potatoes.

'I'm not telling anyone outside of the family,' Stephen adds. 'It's not that I don't trust Ivan – but I don't want word to spread. I don't want any nasty surprises.'

Katica reaches across the table for her son's hand. In that moment, the weight of his decision to emigrate hits him. Over the last years, Stephen has risked his life so many times, choosing togetherness with his family over his own wellbeing. As the prospect of leaving becomes ever more real, so does the realisation that he is bidding farewell to them.

I have always been grateful to have the ability to express myself through music. It is one of the greatest gifts in my life. I think it beautiful to have a musical record of my journey; emotions and experiences captured and turned into song, to be remembered and replayed. Sometimes the true meaning of a song only presents itself with hindsight, the artist's subconscious shimmering forebodingly through the lyrics. On other occasions, the writer feels a burning desire to pin down a feeling in real time. With an overwhelming sense of purpose and immediacy, the artist rushes to their instrument and starts feverishly creating.

That evening, Stephen rushes to the upright piano in his apartment. He has something to say. Seeking closure, he writes a song of leaving. Pouring out all his frustrations, the last piece of music my grandfather composes in his homeland is a bitter-sweet ode to it. 'Farewell to Budapest' is cathartic to write – the honest, loving and critical words flow easily and find their way seamlessly onto its melody:

Life was good here, once upon a time, but now and up until the day I leave, I am nothing but a guest in my own country, my grandfather summarises the lyrics to 'Farewell to Budapest' in the tapes.

He is pleased with the song. It is recorded and a release date is set. But the publisher pulls the release in a last-minute panic, deeming the lyrics too critical. The censorship of his farewell is the last insult Stephen will suffer before he leaves his country.

Now unfortunately this whole thing was censored, so it wasn't published, but I've got the song here with me in England.

It is ironic that 'Farewell to Budapest' is the only song I cannot find amid the many cassette tapes and piles of sheet music. Other than Stephen's reference and description of it in the tapes, I have no record of it. Perhaps it will surface over time, but for now, in a way, it remains censored.

On a damp November morning, all the family come together in secret to see Stephen off at the airport. There have been so many fearful and uncertain goodbyes of late. This one is different. As they hold one another, there is a shared trepidation, but equally, a sense of self-determination that makes all the difference.

After the last goodbyes, squeezing of hands and kissing of cheeks, Stephen leaves to board the plane. He turns the corner, following fellow passengers as they shuffle out of the terminal building. As soon as he turns his back on his parents, brothers and sister, his head fills with worry. In this moment, Stephen is so consumed with fear of the journey ahead that the destination gets obscured. He struggles to picture his new life in England with his wife and child. It seems so far away. Suddenly, the journey ahead appears risky. *What if something goes wrong?* is the intrusive, yet understandable thought circling his mind. Every step now feels both meaningful and laborious. He concentrates on placing one foot in front of the other as he ascends the stairs to the aircraft. As he turns to look back one last time, his feelings of worry vanish in an instant. Instead, a joy washes over Stephen.

All my family stood on the terrace. I waved back to them.

Stephen commits the moment to his mind. He will call upon this memory time and time again. It is such a happy picture, his brothers and his sister, his mother and father, all smiles and well wishes, as he bids farewell to Budapest.

It is not a grand escape nor is it a particularly happy ending. Rather, it is a sentimental goodbye to what was and what could have been if life had played out in a different key.

As Stephen reclines in his seat on the plane, worry begins to creep back into the corners of his mind. All the recent terror still pulsating through him, Stephen focuses on his surroundings, not trusting that he is safe and that his escape will be successful. This is a Russian plane and the Russian pilot and crew dressed in civilian clothing are making him feel uneasy. He only notices how tense he has been throughout the flight when the wheels of the plane hit the runway in Prague and his fists unclench. From here, he has to change onto a connecting flight. It takes a while to disembark. The Russian crew escort him to his terminal. He tries to be subtle each time he glances over his shoulder to see if he is being followed. At any point, Stephen still fears his journey could be derailed yet again, as it has been so many times before.

Finally, it is time to board the connecting flight from Prague to London. An intense knot in his stomach loosens as the crew greet him on board the aircraft. He takes his seat. The wheels of the KLM flight lift off the ground and Stephen finally exhales.

Only when it took off did I feel that I am at last free and that I have made it. I made it to start a new life.

CHAPTER 24

To Those of You Listening

In the early months of 1949, Aladar and Edith's father arrange for a moving van and fill it with an assortment of remaining portraits, furniture and trinkets, soon to be remnants of a bygone era. Taking centre stage among the treasures is the piano. Just before the communist takeover of Hungary, the baby grand Blüthner makes its journey from a burnt-out building in Budapest to a council house on the outskirts of Stratford–upon-Avon. Here, it starts a new life, playing a song of its player's survival.

But I'm not going to record this life, because most of you know already how we lived and what we've done and what happened to us in our new country, Britain.

One story is shared from life after Budapest. It is the mid-sixties and Stephen and Edith are in London, taking a seat at the table in a bustling Italian restaurant. They are treating themselves to a meal after a long day of buying wholesale items for their shop back in Stratford-upon-Avon. In the crowded room, a travelling band entertains the guests, manoeuvring instruments around busy waiters. As Stephen looks back and forth from the menu to the band, he notices that the violinist is staring at him intently.

'What is he looking at?' Stephen mumbles under his breath to Edith, directing her gaze towards the man. To their surprise, he smiles and walks towards them.

'I know you!' he exclaims, grinning widely at Stephen.

A moment passes in which Stephen tries and fails to place the man's face.

'I was the little boy who brought you cigarettes in Sopron camp.'

Stephen is dumbfounded. He stares at the man, then at Edith, before finally realising he's still clutching the menu in his hands. He emphatically puts it down and turns towards the man in recognition. Behind the lines in his face, he sees the youthful boy who dipped in and out of the camp, undetected by the guards, inspiring Stephen to do the same.

'This is amazing!' he says. 'How did you recognise me?'

'It's your eyes – you have a certain look,' the man says.

To those of you listening . . . I sit up straight as my grandfather addresses me directly, through time and space via this old cassette recording. *I am sorry for how I have told these events . . . I am not a professional storyteller.*

I break out into an involuntary, loud, cathartic laugh: what a rare moment of false modesty from my grandfather, whom I've got to know, at least posthumously, through his storytelling and his music. This is how my grandfather finishes his story:

Today's date is the second of February 1987. I'm concluding this tape, which I made for a future generation.

The tape clicks, and I instinctively know what's about to happen. Before it does, I hear in my mind the first words I ever heard him speak: *My darling children, I have finished now my story.*

And then I hear the creak of the piano stool.

Stephen's fingers drape over the keys; the romantic flurry of scales evoke a curtain rising, a cocktail bar; a light-heartedness is mirrored

238

in the quick syncopation of the notes he picks out. I see him as a young man, in his silk shirt and dinner jacket, accompanying a glamorous singer dressed in feathers and sequins.

The flurry of optimism descends into a minor key. The tempo slows and now, those same scales evoke a snow falling, a heaviness filling the space in between the notes. The song almost grinds to a halt until, as if from a distance, the melody of 'Remember Me' breaks through. Introducing this theme fills the air with a euphoria as the melody grows stronger and clearer, like a figure approaching from afar, who turns out to be a dear old friend. When we recognise them, we start to run towards them. The coda is a variation of the theme, playful staccato notes like child's play and then, a flowery crescendo that builds and builds until it reaches its final conclusion and we find home, in song.

Stephen dies eighteen months after committing his story to tape, on 13 August 1988.

Epilogue

With their sharply tailored clothes, thick foreign accents and mysterious pasts, Stephen and Edith would never quite blend in. Life in 1950s Britain would be marred with a different kind of hardship. Always entrepreneurial in spirit, they tried their best to assimilate, to weave their way into society anew. Stephen and Edith worked hard running a restaurant, the Paprika, which boasted Stratford-upon-Avon's first espresso machine. They opened a shop, selling tourist kitsch, called Shakespeare's Doorstep and another, selling drapery and women's fashion, the French-sounding Chez Vivienne. Although life in Stratford-upon-Avon was peaceful, my grandparents never felt entirely welcome and their attempts at social ascension were ultimately stifled. Edith would often lament that, although she frequently made a habit of inviting the neighbours over for dinner, they never seemed to be invited back. Their restaurant, despite its popularity, was never granted a liquor license by the local council.

A combination of having to provide for his family, the daunting task of starting anew and thinly veiled xenophobia prevented Stephen from pursuing a music career in his newly elected home. Of course, he never stopped playing or composing and his talents were undeniable. The neighbours' suspicion quickly turned into reverence as Stephen's beautiful piano playing engulfed the evening air. On most nights, he would play his compositions on the Blüthner piano, lulling the neighbourhood into the night. My dad loved falling asleep to his dad's playing and I in turn loved falling asleep to his. I cherish the memory of it and keep it together with my most precious collection of experiences.

There is one TV appearance on ITV Midlands, on which Stephen was a musical guest – a show called *Rainbow Room*, hosted by popular children's TV presenter Jean Morton. I have a recording of this performance. My dad never liked it, reacting instinctively to what he perceived as condescension towards his father. As I listen to it, I know what he means.

'That was something typically Hungarian, wasn't it?' Jean asks him in a bouncy Queen's English. Her tone conveys that, to her, the man behind the piano and the music he plays are foreign, above anything else.

'Yes,' Stephen obliges somewhat awkwardly, before adding, 'I composed it for this show especially.'

'Oh that's nice,' she says, and I shudder.

As much as it is the narrative in my family, I don't think Stephen spent much of his time regretting his life decisions. In the tapes, he makes a point of saying that a move to America would not have necessarily resulted in a successful music career and that being with his family was always the priority. Be that as it may, Julie recalls how her father would often point at the credits whenever they watched movies together: 'I know him!' was the mantra as Stephen looked upon the names of Hungarian composers and producers who, unlike him, had taken the plunge and moved to the USA. In those moments, sleepy Stratford-upon-Avon must have seemed so very far away from Hollywood.

*   *   *

'It's strange.' Julie examines her thoughts after reading a draft of an early chapter. 'You write about my father so beautifully, but you paint him in a kind of romanticised light . . . That's not really how I remember him.'

'But darling,' my mother interjects, drawing out the last word with her strong German accent, 'that chapter was before all the trauma.'

'Yes, I know,' Julie replies, her eyes still fixed upon the invisible. It takes her a moment to reconcile the man she knew with the protagonist of this story.

It must be a strange sensation, having her father come back to life through the eyes of another. She stares so intensely into the distance, I feel as though I too can see her thoughts. This interaction inspires me to examine how I have portrayed my grandfather. Over the following days, the thoughts percolate as Christmas approaches. It was always my intention not to edit Stephen's harsher tones – my grandfather and his arrogance, his self-belief and his roughness. Of course, he has come alive in this book through me. This story is a reflection of Stephen. Like in music, when one artist brings another's work back to life, the performance will have a different inflection, although it is the same song.

Undoubtedly, though, Istvan Bastyai was a very different person to Stephen de Bastion. It is inevitable that we change throughout our lives, regardless of whether our horizons are pretty and predictable or full of extreme heights and depths. Stephen's experiences during the Holocaust left him with a lot of rage. It would come out in loud, gruff spouts of Hungarian, which may have been harmless in meaning, but to Richard and Julie, the harsh tones of their parents' secret language could sometimes be terrifying. Particularly sensitive to the cold and to any smells vaguely reminding him of sulphur and smoke, Stephen would be provoked into barked orders and statements such as 'close the window' and 'the egg stinks' – incidentally, these are two of just a few phrases of Hungarian that have filtered down to my generation.

It is Elizabeth and Peter, the children from Edith's first marriage with Laslo Somogyi, who perhaps experienced Stephen at his worst and bore the brunt of his harshest tones. Peter is not even called Peter. Peter's real name is Stephen. I don't remember how old I was when I learned this, but I remember that it blew my mind. Apparently, with the arrival of the new man of the house, there was only room for one Stephen, so Edith's son was made to go by his middle name. I can't help but feel that this is all one really needs to know to get a sense of the size of my grandfather's ego. It would cast long shadows and reflects the overall reception Edith's children received from their stepfather.

After Aladar passed away in 1955, Katica moved to England to live with her son and his family. My dad held many visceral memories of Katica in the last years of her life. They paint a sad picture and one that I recognise from reading other stories of Holocaust survivors. Displaced souls, alive, but sick with bereavement, detached from all they knew. It is a song of silent suffering, a slow and painful lament of identities lost and experiences endured. It is such a rudely unglamorous closing act for strong and artistic Katica. In England, she reaches old age, but it brings a sorrowful loneliness. Isolated by language and culture, she spent most of her days chain-smoking in her room above the restaurant. With nicotine-stained fingers, she would grab the handle of her walking stick and hammer the floorboards beneath to call for her working family below. Sometimes she would play at the piano, rheumatic fingers fumbling over the keys, grafting through a feeble waltz. In those days, Katica found an unlikely friend in Peter. They both so appreciated having someone to speak to in their mother tongue, having someone with whom to connect over their lost home.

Everyone in the newly named de Bastion household carried a burden and, without the language around or greater understanding of what they were dealing with, suffered in solitude. Late in life, Edith once confessed to my mother that she had a recurring dream. Almost every night, she would sit on the stoop of an apartment house in Budapest as faceless, uniformed soldiers came to take her away.

I do not wish to know what Stephen's nightmares were made of.

Going through another box of photographs with my sister, I come across a couple of gorgeous pictures of a New Year's Eve party in Stratford-upon-Avon. Stephen and Edith are posing in the middle of a group shot with three friends – all smiles, champagne flutes and party hats. Edith shines in these photos. Her dark hair, pinned in an up-do, is in beautiful contrast to her porcelain skin. She's wearing a chunky bracelet around her upper arm, making her look particularly youthful. With her broad smile, she looks as happy as she does cool. Peering up from behind her, Stephen wears a smirk that shows all his other shades – my grandfather and his charm, his sense of humour, his warmth and his wit. We are complex creatures and Stephen is no exception. As I look at the Stephen captured in this moment, I feel certain that I've got the balance right.

She didn't need to, but a couple of days after our conversation, Julie pulls me aside to tell me that she thinks it is beautiful, how I am reflecting Stephen, that I have her blessing, and that I should continue to follow my heart and my instinct.

Throughout this entire process, I have felt so grateful to have the cassette tapes. Hearing Stephen tell his story, growing familiar with his voice with all its inflexions and inferences, has been a truly incredible experience. The greatest gift is to know he wanted his story told. Not long after I start the journey, Stephen interrupts tales of his mother's childhood and addresses the listener directly. His tone is light, the last word falling into laughter.

I hope you're not just humouring me to keep me busy. I hope you're actually going to use this for something.

Many attempts across generations have been made to receive compensation for what happened to my family. In the early 1990s, both my dad and Peter tried and failed to get Hungary to give back the stolen property in Budapest. With the help of the Jewish Claims Office, they went through long and tedious court cases. In the end, my dad was offered the equivalent of 250 euros as compensation for the apartment block in St Stephen's Square in central Budapest. He declined.

Germany refused to compensate our family for the apartment buildings Aladar's father Jakab Holtzer owned in Berlin, citing his son Emil's debt and supposed criminal record as the main reason why compensation wasn't due.

It is estimated that around a quarter of a million Germans were directly involved in the murder of Jews, and that is not taking into account the millions of soldiers and civilians in allied countries who readily joined in. But genocide requires the active consent of millions. With so many perpetrators and beneficiaries of the Holocaust, the true value of what was lost is impossible to quantify or repay. Some people advanced in their careers, taking vacant jobs of Jews who were forcibly removed from their positions, and others bought formerly Jewish-owned real estate and businesses at cheap prices without ever facing a consequence – stolen wealth, trickling down through the generations.

Most Holocaust perpetrators were never put on trial for their crimes. While a handful of high-profile Nazis were tried in the immediate aftermath at the Nuremburg trials, the majority were never brought to justice. Most of them were simply absorbed back into society and continued their lives, retaining their personal and professional positions.

For survivors of the Holocaust and their children, there is no justice, even for those who do receive compensation. There is no justice in a world in which the political pendulum is once again swinging ever further towards the far right. While court cases against Germany and Hungary by Jewish survivors continue to this day, antisemitism and general ignorance is on the rise across the globe. How can there be justice if the crimes committed are largely being erased from our history books and our collective consciousness? In 2019, the *Guardian* reported on the findings of a poll commissioned by the Holocaust Memorial Trust in the UK. It found that one in twenty British adults do not believe that the Holocaust even happened. A similar survey found that one in ten young Americans (aged between eighteen and thirty-nine) either believed the Holocaust to be a myth or had never even heard of it.

It is a couple of weeks prior to completing the first draft of this book. I am sitting in the back of a taxi, heading to Marylebone station. The driver is chatty and friendly. He is originally from Albania, but he tells me that he and his family have lived in the UK for nearly twenty years. I am about to ask him whether he still feels welcome here, given the increased anti-immigrant rhetoric permeating the country, but before I get a chance to do so, he says, in all seriousness and out of the blue: 'It's a shame Hitler's not around anymore.'

At first, I am certain I have misheard. I place my hand on the headrest of the passenger seat in front of me, and do not attempt to hide the confusion and shock written across my face.

'Uhm . . . what did you say?'

'He was a strong leader! You know, we need people like that now . . .'

Referring to the Russian invasion of Ukraine, which we had covered in our small talk five minutes prior, he adds: 'If Hitler were alive and in charge today, he could really put Russia in its place.'

'But he did murder six million Jews.' I try to deliver the statement more like a comedian would a punchline.

'Yes, well, every country has its plus and minus points,' he replies.

I fall back into my seat and say: 'Hitler put my grandfather in a concentration camp.' My words come out childlike and seem to come from a place within I do not recognise.

The driver is stunned into silence. I can see in his eyes that he is struck with what I chose to believe is empathy, though perhaps, it is embarrassment. He clearly hadn't expected to be confronted with someone personally affected by the subject matter. In this moment, we conveniently pull into my destination.

'Perhaps it's just as well that we're here,' I laugh, trying to break the tension.

'You know,' I open the door and unbuckle my seatbelt, 'Hitler did invade Russia . . . it didn't go well for him.'

He didn't know that and says that I should go visit the North London café where his wife works for a free coffee, but I never do.

*　　*　　*

EPILOGUE

The Blüthner piano sat in the living room of a terraced house in Stratford-upon-Avon as my dad, Richard, and his little sister Julie were raised to be as English as possible. My dad never learned to speak Hungarian, or what it meant to be Jewish, but he did learn to play on that piano, a delicate tune of defiance, continuing the de Bastion tradition in his own way. It was the sixties and Richard's black-and-white post-war Britain burst into colour with the arrival of rock 'n' roll. Although he encouraged and expected his son to take piano lessons, Stephen was less approving of electric keyboards and the twelve-bar blues. The cultural shift of the 1960s widened the chasm between Richard and Julie's generation and that of their parents, resulting in constant friction. Stephen eventually put his foot down and forced Richard to quit his rock 'n' roll band, fearing that playing music with those long-haired boys was too much of a distraction from academia. The band, Terry Webb and the Spiders, continued without Richard. It featured a certain John Bonham on drums; John would go on to form a group called Led Zeppelin. My dad told me stories of their first gigs being shut down by police, who pulled the plug on their instruments. Un-amplified, John Bonham would continue thrashing his drums, solo-ing long into the night. Fulfilling his father's wish, just as Stephen had his, Richard went to university instead to studied geology, something vaguely respectable in the eyes of his family.

Stephen was not an encouraging teacher or fellow musician. His battle scars were too deep and his ego too bruised. That's the thing about reverb: what makes a harmony even more beautiful makes a misstep seem all the more jarring; the uncomfortable notes linger for much longer than they should. I wish he could have found joy in my dad's passion, and I wish he could have given him a little more freedom.

The piano yearned for freedom, too. It was given to my dad after Stephen passed away and was moved to Berlin in the 1990s, only miles from where it started its journey nearly exactly one hundred years earlier. My dad had moved to the utopian island of West Berlin in the seventies to pursue a career in music, not with a piano, but with a guitar, played left handed, upside down like Jimi Hendrix.

The piano had at least geographically come full circle and, as it arrived, it was the Iron not the Velvet curtain that fell. The Berlin Wall collapsed as I learned to walk and started to play my first notes on that piano in a world that was opening up. I was a third-generation survivor and a girl, with the great fortune of growing up in a small corner of the world that was liberal and kind. The piano experienced a renaissance with decades of love, songwriting, performing and recording. My dad was my biggest champion. He encouraged my music and poured all of his love into us, his family, the piano and all the many friends who played upon it.

September 2019. My dad is dying, but he is radiating life. We were told in February that his cancer was back and that this time he was, unequivocally, terminal. 'Aren't we all?' was his response, as he proceeded to fill his diary with music and adventures. One, in particular, is of importance to this story.

My dad's cousin Judit, Annie's daughter, has organised something very special: a family reunion in Hungary with twenty-five people, most of whom I've never met, all related by Katica's side of the family.

I fly to Budapest from London to meet my dad, sister and Aunt Julie, who have taken the train from Berlin. We stay in the Bastion hotel for one night – no relation, just a quirk of fate and a little, generational joke. In the evening, we indulge in traditional Hungarian cuisine in a restaurant around the corner from the hotel. When the waiter comes to take our order, my dad orders his food and chats with the waiter in a free-flowing Hungarian.

'Well, it's in there somewhere!' He shrugs and smiles as we all look at him in amazement. Apparently, all it took for the secret language to unlock was for him to return to the fatherland.

The following morning we explore the city by taxi. We briefly ask the car to stop so that we can walk around St Stephen's Square. Unlike the many tourists, we look away from the cathedral, up towards the third-floor apartment of the residential building. I should feel something, looking up at the glorious apartment in the heart of Budapest that once belonged to my family. I should feel the pang of injustice at all that was stolen and never returned. But in that moment, all I can think about is that I'm soon to experience a much greater loss than that of family wealth.

In the afternoon, we meet Judit and have coffee in her home in Budapest. It is a traditional pre-war apartment. The dining table is covered with an old-fashioned lace tablecloth and the walls are lined with paintings similar to the ones at home in Berlin. I feel a sense of belonging here. There is something about this apartment in Budapest that feels familiar to me, truly, as though I have been here before in a dream.

At this point in time, I am unfamiliar with Stephen's story, but reliving the memory, I realise that, as I step over the threshold and into Judit's apartment, I am standing on the same spot where Stephen collapsed upon his return from surviving the concentration camps.

Together with Judit, we drive to Bànk, where the family gathering is taking place, and the following morning people start arriving.

Everyone is excited. Some live in Hungary and haven't travelled far, others have flown in from Sweden, from France and some from as far away as Australia. I recognise most of the faces, even though I'm meeting these people for the first time. I recognise Katica's delicate, heart-shaped face, her small, dark brown eyes and her wavy hair in her descendants. We sit in a large circle in the living room and decide to go around the room introducing ourselves and saying a little about what we do. As we start, it becomes clear that we have more in common than our small physical frames and heart-shaped faces. Without fail, each one of us has dedicated our lives to either music or humanitarian sciences, or a combination of the two. I start to question the very concept of free will by the time we're halfway around the room. Our connection to one another is palpable and it feels gloriously defiant. 'What sort of people had we been?' I hear Stephen's voice echoing in my head as I think upon this extraordinary experience.

'We still are these people,' I reply quietly under my breath.

In the evening, we have dinner together in a nearby hotel – the kind that Stephen would have played at. Judit has booked a small function room for us that has a piano. After the meal, Karen, one of the Australian branch, unpacks her violin. My dad sits at the piano and I sit next to him. We come together in music, singing a medley of our compositions. As Karen plays a beautiful solo on one of my dad's songs as if they've been playing together for decades, I look out into the room and feel overcome with a deep, primal feeling of peace and satisfaction, an ancestral sigh of relief that we are here and together. We exist and we're singing.

'Stephen de Bastion: Songs From *The Piano Player of Budapest*' is a 12-track album, lovingly created by Roxanne de Bastion to accompany this book. The album sees Roxanne restore, re-record and re-imagine her grandfather's music, working from a treasure trove of cassette tapes of his recordings, as well as original sheet music. The album is available digitally, on CD and vinyl. Follow the QR code or visit Roxanne's website for details:

roxannedebastion.com

Note on Writing

This is a true story based on Stephen's verbal and written retelling of events, underpinned by other source material such as documents, memoirs by other family members, photo albums, conversations with family members and history books. Both Stephen's verbal and written accounts are rich in detail, including names, places, dates and even bits of dialogue. Occasionally, I have added a touch of my own storytelling to colour in the details.

Acknowledgements

How I came to write this book is a truly magical story. On 29 March 2021, I published a string of tweets briefly outlining the survival story of my grandfather and his piano along with the hashtag 'International Piano Day'. It was spontaneous and I thought nothing of it. Two days later, though, I received a message that would be life-changing:

Hi – I'm a literary agent at Morgan Green Creatives and loved your piano story – I wondered if you had thought of writing a book? Would love to chat more if this interested you. Kirsty

For finding me and this story and for so elegantly guiding me through the process, I'd like to thank my agent Kirsty McLachlan. I didn't know how much I needed to write this book until you presented me with the opportunity to do so.

For seeing potential in this book and making it a reality, I would like to thank my editor Emma Smith, as well as everyone at Little, Brown. You have all made me feel that this very personal story is in safe and sensitive hands. For bringing this book to the USA, I'd like to thank Jessica Case at Pegasus Books. And for bringing it to Hungary, I'd like to say köszönöm szépen to Barbara Besze at Lira Books.

I acknowledge that this is not just my story to tell. For giving me their blessings to share it, I thank my family with all my heart. I have felt an immense pressure to get it right and I hope you feel happy with how I have told our story. A special thank you goes to my Aunt Julie, my sister Geraldine and my mum Susanne, as well as to Judit, Peter and Liz. You have all helped me shape this story by sharing your thoughts, feelings and memories with me and I'm very grateful for all your help and support.

Another special thank you goes to my Cousin Nicole, without whom it simply would not have been possible to share Stephen's story in such detail. It was she who prompted Stephen to record his story for prosperity and for that I am forever truly grateful.

Speaking of family, I'd like to thank my partner Shaun for being such a huge support. A gifted writer himself, he was always first to read each chapter and indulged me in hours of late-night chats and discussions over things I was researching, thinking, feeling and discovering. I should probably also thank him for tolerating me taking over our shared office.

For providing encouragement and access to their archives, I'd like to thank the Wiener Holocaust Library in London. It was a beautiful place to research and write in, and I recommend readers to pay it a visit. I also recommend my Uncle Lorant's book, *Memoirs of a Master Falconer* (published posthumously as a limited edition by the British Falconry Archive in 2014). It provided rich detail for this story and is a delightful read, in which Lorant's blinkered love for nature, wildlife and birds, particularly birds of prey, outshine the hardships suffered during the war.

I would like to acknowledge my dad's beautiful, unpublished autobiography *Almost English*, which is essentially the sequel to this story and an important inspiration to me. My sister and I hope to get it published one day soon.

And on that note, musical pun intended, I give my biggest thanks to my beloved dad, for guiding me still.

Index

INDEX

education 10–13
forced labour 67–73
    in Mauthausen concentration camp 163,
        165, 166–8
    in Russia xx–xxi, 84–6, 89–97, 99–104,
        105–11, 113
    in Sopron ghetto 154–6, 158–9, 161, 168,
        211, 238
    and Gunskirchen concentration camp 168,
        169, 170–5, 179–83
Hungarian accent 191
and Hungarian anti-Semitism 30–2, 61, 150,
    151–2
internships 13–14
journey back to Hungary from Gunskirchen
    185–90
journey home from the Russian front 103–4,
    105–11, 113–19, 120–6, 127–35
and the legacy of the Holocaust 243–4, 249
letters 105, 110–11
and life in England 237–8, 241–5
in Mauthausen concentration camp 162,
    163–8
military training call-up 66
and music 3, 4, 11–12, 14–15, 17
    after the war 215–16
    dress shirts 147, 158
    in England 241–2
    guest on the *Rainbow Room* 242
    in Italy 48–9
    Kekes contract 79–83
    love of music 39, 75
    partnership with Alvia Suli 32–4, 63–4,
        67, 77
    plays piano in bars 5–6, 18–19, 143–4
    plays piano in Switzerland 25–8, 29–30,
        31, 34–8, 41–8, 71
    plays piano on train journey back from
        Russia 129–33
    radio performances 230
    and reading music 26–7
    recordings of his piano playing 22–3,
        238–9
    sheet music of 22, 37–8
    work with lyricists 76
musical compositions 47, 75, 76, 148–9,
    226–7, 241–2
    'A Fire Red Rose' 216
    'An Old Mill is Dreaming' xix, xx, 111,
        144
    'Emlékszel Meg' ('Remember Me') 223–7,
        230, 239
    'Farewell to Budapest' 234

for *Help, I Inherited!* 19–23, 28, 134
for *Lady of Promise* (Igéret Hölgeje) 230–1
'Sleep, Sleep, Little Boy' 231
for *Temporarily Poor* 28
'Up and Down the Scale of Life' 14–15
narrative reliability 152–3
offered US citizenship by American liberators
    181
original family name 'Bastyai Holtzer' xxi
physical strength/fitness of 69–70, 121
relationships
    first wife, Baba 3, 17–18, 41
    Irene Agay 18–22, 31–2
    Magda 143–4, 147, 155–9
    Roszi 28–30, 32, 41–2, 44, 64–5
    second wife, Edith 72, 141–4, 213–14,
        215–17, 227, 229–31, 233, 245
returns to Hungary from Italy 49, 63–5
sporty 13
suffers difficult birth 7
suffers health complications following the war
    213
suffers illnesses during ordeals 102–3, 122–3,
    125
tape recordings xviii–xxii, 7, 38–9, 76, 102,
    105, 111, 113, 115, 126, 129, 138, 142,
    144, 150, 163, 185, 218, 220, 225,
    229–30, 238–9, 242, 246
thirty-ninth birthday 216–17
de Bastion (née Hoffman), Susanne (Stephen's
    daughter-in-law) xi, xiv, 8–9, 191–2,
    243
Deak Ferenc Street, Szeged 57
death camps 149, 154, 202
    see also Auschwitz
death marches 161–2, 164, 168–9, 175
Debrecen 134, 215
Denmark Street, London 14
Dix Publishing Group 14
Don, River 96, 99, 108, 139
Doroshevich 107
Dunacorzo, The (restaurant) 33–4, 63, 67, 73,
    77, 116
dysentery 102–3, 122

Eastern Front 107, 109–10
Eichmann, Adolf 146
Ellington, Duke 83
Emma (play) 18
Ents 168

far right politics 67, 108, 146, 247
Favor, Mr 43–7

263

INDEX